THE UNIQUENESS
MYTH

and other
misconceptions
that derail businesses

Dale Furtwengler

Peregrine Press
St. Louis, Missouri

Library of Congress Catalog-In-Publication Data

Furtwengler, Dale
     The Uniqueness Myth and other misconceptions that
     derail businesses / Dale Furtwengler
     p.   cm.
     Includes index
     ISBN 0-9661478-2-0
     Management

Library of Congress Control Number: 2003195002

This book is dedicated to business leaders

at all levels in the organization

who strive continuously to increase their skills

and their company's success.

Contents

Introduction

Business leaders are faced with two conflicting realities:

1. There are things that every business must do to be successful, regardless of industry
2. There are nuances to every industry

This dichotomy complicates decision making. It forces leaders to choose between the industry's traditional wisdom and ideas proffered by the general business community. How do they resolve this dilemma?

Experience has taught me that most business leaders choose the traditional industry approach. Why? They feel that their industry is different, *unique*.

While it's true that there are nuances to every industry, my experience has been that leaders who get distracted by these nuances often get into trouble. Conversely, leaders who focus on the things every business must do to be successful, enjoy exceptional success. You don't have to take my word for it; there's ample evidence to support this claim.

Jack Welch, retired Chairman/CEO of General Electric, said "finding **the better way, the best idea, from whomever will share it with us,** has become our central focus". [1]

Patrick Kelly, who took PSS/World Medical, Inc. from start up to $1 billion in revenues in 15 years, said, "I don't think I've ever had an original idea in my life. At PSS, all the great

---

[1] General Electric 1997 Annual Report

ones were borrowed from somebody else, or were created by people in a branch, then adopted by the whole company." [2]

Finally, there are countless business leaders who dramatically improved their organizations' effectiveness by benchmarking the best practices of *non-competing* firms. That's right; they benchmarked firms outside their industry.

Jack Welch, Patrick Kelly and all the leaders who benchmark other firms, share a common trait; they see the similarities in business rather than the differences. They recognize industry nuances, yet choose to focus their energy on the things *every* business must do to be successful. That's one of the keys to their success. It can be the key to yours as well.

The Uniqueness Myth is designed to help you discover the universal truths that drive every successful business. The more familiar you become with these truths, the less likely you are to be distracted by the nuances of your industry. If you succumb to these distractions (most of us do from time to time), *The Uniqueness Myth* also serves as a ready reference to help you refocus your attention where it needs to be.

How will you know when you've strayed from these truths? When you try a number of different approaches and none of them produce the result you desire. Lack of results often indicates that it's time to revisit the universal truths.

The Uniqueness Myth isn't the only misconception business leaders suffer. False impressions exist in every aspect of business. Here are a few examples to whet your appetite:

---

[2] Patrick Kelly, *Faster Company*, Wiley & Sons 1998, page 31

- Low prices are an effective strategy for the vast majority of businesses
- Mergers are effective in lowering costs
- Production cost measures help companies achieve lower costs
- Profitable businesses are successful

Leaders who are unaware of these misconceptions will, at best, limit their companies' success; at worst, they'll cause their companies' demise.

There are many reasons why 80% of the businesses in the United States fail. *The Uniqueness Myth* identifies those reasons and offers alternatives that will help you take your company beyond survival to industry leadership.

Whether you're a business owner, professional manager or someone who aspires to leadership, *The Uniqueness Myth* is designed to make it easier for you and your company to enjoy greater success and a more financially rewarding future.

Dale Furtwengler

Acknowledgments

I have been blessed to have many people in my life who have shared their love, wisdom and experience with me. I'd like to say a special thank you to those involved in this project.

Charlotte Furtwengler, my wife, a constant source of love and support.

Charles and Johanna Furtwengler, my parents, whose love and encouragement laid the foundation for my success.

Mr. Francois Rijk, Rijk Consulting, who helped me understand why I wasn't happy with my early efforts.

Ms. Cindy Boling, a dear friend and client, at whose behest I embarked on a writing career.

Mr. Andy Klemm, Klemm & Associates, and Ms. Wendy Gauntt, CIO Services, whose insights and encouragement have been invaluable.

Ms. Dorothy Connor, a wonderfully caring and gifted editor.

Ms. Kare Anderson, Say It Better Center, who helped me clarify the theme of *The Uniqueness Myth*.

Ms. Lori Keller and the team at The Snap Group for the wonderful job they did on the cover.

To all of you, I extend my heartfelt thanks.

SQUEEZED FOR TIME?

Time-Saving Tips

I know that the demands on your time are incredible today; that's why I've written this book in modular form. Each chapter covers a different aspect of business – strategy, marketing, selling, production, finance, etc. This format was chosen to provide:

1. Quick access to the issues most important to your company's success
2. The core concept that's often overlooked when business leaders get distracted by the unique aspects of their business
3. Other misconceptions about that chapter's topic

Quick Access

You don't have to read the whole book. When you know which aspect of your operation needs attention, go directly to that chapter and get the information you need to move your organization to a higher level of success.

Each chapter is organized as follows:

1. Core concept definition box
2. Core concept discussion
3. Other misconceptions discussion
4. Executive summary

You don't have to search for the core concept; it's in a box at the very beginning of the chapter. A detailed discussion of the core concept appears immediately below the box.

Other misconceptions are separated from the core concept section to avoid confusion. I want you to be aware of these misconceptions, but I don't want them to distract you from the core concept.

Finally, I've created an executive summary to give you the essence of the chapter. If you're not sure which chapter is relevant to your company's situation, the executive summary provides a quick overview of each chapter's content.

Core Concept

The core concept listed in the box at the beginning of each chapter is the universal truth about that aspect of business. It's the premise that holds true regardless of whether you're in the business of dry cleaning clothes or manufacturing jet engines, whether you're serving individuals or businesses, whether you're a one-person shop or a Fortune 100 company.

When your business is struggling, generally it's because you've lost sight of one or more of the core concepts. Any time that your company is floundering, revisit the appropriate chapter and refocus your company on that chapter's core concept. You'll be amazed at how quickly difficult situations turn around when you're focused on the core concept.

Other Misconceptions

The Uniqueness Myth isn't the only business myth that exists. There are myths about every aspect of business as you'll see. Each chapter contains a discussion of these myths in the *Other Misconceptions* section. Just don't let them distract you from the core concept.

Executive Summary

Whether you're looking for affirmation of what you know or trying to determine which chapter addresses your company's current situation, the executive summary can help. It also serves as a quick review which is important; I've packed a lot of information into each chapter.

I hope that the book's format and these time-saving tips will help you gain useful insights more quickly than you might with other formats. I want you to get the most from every investment you make including your investment in this book.

Dale Furtwengler

STRATEGY:

There are two approaches to dealing with the future – create it or react to it.

Which will you choose?

1

Business Strategy

What is the key to every successful business strategy?

**To provide something the market wants or needs
that it isn't getting.**

Core Concept – Unique Offering

If you're not offering prospective customers something new
and exciting, what's their incentive to buy from you? Would
you shift your business from a trusted supplier to a stranger
without getting something new?

You may be thinking, "I would if I got a lower price." A lower price is something new, isn't it? It's something you weren't getting before. In fact, this is the way many business owners choose to differentiate their offerings from their competitors' offerings. How effective is this strategy? Here are three perspectives on the use of a low-price strategy:

- The low-price dilemma
- Successful low-price strategies
- Unique offerings

The Low-Price Dilemma

Competing on price is often successful in the early years of a company's operations because overhead is low. As sales increase so do costs. You hire more people, add inventory, buy equipment, rent more space and finance the additional receivables and inventory.

Since most business owners don't enjoy cost control, these overhead costs often grow to levels at least as high, if not higher, than what's normal for the industry. These owners find themselves trying to cover higher costs with low profit margins. It's a Catch-22 situation. To understand why, place yourself in the shoes of this business owner.

You know that you need to raise prices to cover your higher overhead. You also know that low prices are what attracted your customers in the first place. If you raise prices you risk losing your customers. If you don't, you're going to work very hard for little, if any, return.

The only other option is to cut costs and you really don't enjoy that, which means you're probably not very good at it either. How's that for an ugly set of alternatives?

What will most business owners in this situation do? They'll try to cut costs. They'll point to Wal-Mart and Southwest Airlines and say, "We can do that!"

The reality is that the Wal-Marts and Southwests of the world are rare. These companies hire people who get a *thrill* from outperforming their competitors. They enjoy accomplishing more with less. While most companies strive for low costs because they *must,* Wal-Mart and Southwest do it because it *excites* them.

The psychological difference between necessity and desire can be seen in the *consistency* of the low cost structure that Wal-Mart and Southwest maintain. Companies that don't possess a passion for low cost go through cycles of hiring and firing large numbers of people depending on which direction the economic wind is blowing. With ample evidence of this in the workings of many Fortune 500 companies, is it any wonder that owners of smaller businesses fall victim to this misconception?

Let's assume that as a business owner you are unaware of the psychological difference between desire and necessity, much less their ability to impact cost cutting. You embark on a cost-cutting effort.

If you're only modestly successful, which is typically the case, you're back to your original dilemma, raising prices to customers who value low prices vs. working for little if any return. You'll spend countless hours vacillating between the alternatives, raising prices and cutting costs. This cycle of weighing unpleasant alternatives creates a dizzying eddy that traps you. Your inability to make a decision often results in the situation worsening to the point that the business fails.

The low-price dilemma arises when a business uses low prices to attract customers, but allows its overhead to grow to a level that's "normal" for the industry.

You can avoid this dilemma by differentiating your offerings without resorting to lower prices. If, however, your heart is really set on using a low-price strategy, let's learn from those who employ it successfully.

Successful Low-Price Strategies
Wal-Mart and Southwest Airlines have successfully used a low price strategy for years. Wal-Mart uses an extensive database to track customers' buying habits. This helps them minimize their inventory investment and its attendant storage, handling, insurance and interest costs.

Southwest Airlines' ability to turn a plane around more quickly than any other airline in the industry has been a big factor in controlling their costs.

These are just two examples of how Wal-Mart and Southwest maintain consistently low costs. The key is that both have a passion for outperforming their competitors. Their superior performance translates into lower costs.

I hope you noticed the language in the previous paragraph. The words "outperforming" and "superior performance" were used intentionally. There is a body of science that studies the impact of language on human behavior; it's called neuro-linguistic programming.

Proponents of neuro-linguistic programming tell us that language that implies gain accelerates goal achievement while language that indicates loss slows, and may even prevent, attainment of your goal. What does that mean in terms of a low-price strategy?

To be successful, a low-price strategy requires a low-cost structure. Neuro-linguistic programming suggests that you focus your organization's attention on being better than your competitors, accomplishing more than they do with fewer resources. When the goal is achieved your employees gain a sense of accomplishment and justifiable pride in the results they helped produce. Let's contrast that with the emotions employees experience when they successfully cut costs.

Did the phrase "successfully cut costs" give you the same sense of satisfaction that "outperforming your competitors" did? Why not? When you cut costs there's a sense of sacrifice. It's like going on a diet. All during the diet you're foregoing something you want. Once you've gotten to your desired weight, what do you do? You reward yourself with the very food that caused your weight problem in the first place. That's what happens with cost-cutting. As soon as you achieve your spending goal, you want to reward yourself by spending more.

Conversely, when you "outperform your competitors", you're *gaining* competitive advantage. There's no loss; you haven't foregone anything. Instead, you experience success and what you want is *more success*. That's why "outperforming your competitors" is a more successful approach than cost-cutting.

A low-price strategy can be effective if you instill in your organization a desire to outperform your competitors.

If this approach isn't attractive to you, there are other ways to make your offerings unique.

Unique Offerings

We spoke earlier of the low-price dilemma. How can you avoid falling into this trap? Determine what the market wants and give it to them; preferably something that they can't get anywhere else.

Easier said than done? Not if you listen to Michael Treacy and Fred Wiersema. In their book, *The Discipline of Market Leaders*, they simplify the process of identifying customer desires by defining three types of buyers; those who value:

- low prices
- product innovation
- customer intimacy

As buyers, we value all three, but in varying degrees. Generally, someone who wants exceptional service isn't going to want the latest technology. Why? New technology is fraught with problems. That's not what someone who values exceptional service wants.

Of course, what we value is influenced by what we are buying. Someone, who values customer intimacy on big ticket items, may go to Wal-Mart for detergents, light bulbs and other household supplies. The question is, "Which buyer should your business serve?"

Treacy and Wiersema tell us that one of the keys to market leadership is identifying which type of buyer best fits your company's capabilities.

- As we've already discussed, if the people in your organization enjoy accomplishing more with less, target the low price buyer.

- If your team's creativity runs more to developing new products/ services than building efficient operating systems, serve buyers who value innovation.
- Do your employees experience a natural high when they see the sparkle in a satisfied customer's eyes? Offer customer intimacy.

It's that simple; what excites the people in your organization dictates which market to serve and how to approach it.

How can we be sure that Treacy and Wiersema's approach works? Let's look at a few success stories. Southwest Airlines serves the low-cost buyer and has experienced the most consistent profits seen in the airline industry since deregulation. Intel's penchant for innovation has allowed it to maintain its industry leadership for decades. Nordstrom's, Ritz-Carlton and PSS/World Medical attribute their financial success to superior customer service.

All of these companies are very successful, in part, because they focus on serving only *one* of the three buyer groups. In doing so they have created a unique offering that meets the needs of the market they serve.

Let your organization's passion and strength determine which market your company should serve.

Combine Treacy and Wiersema's approach with a clear understanding of what the market wants or needs and you've found your formula for success. Your unique offerings will garner higher prices and profit margins than your industry typically enjoys. The additional cash you generate will allow you to increase the already commanding lead you've gained over your competitors.

***For the vast majority of businesses, unique offerings offer
greater profit potential than a low-price strategy.***

The importance of low prices isn't the only misconception
associated with strategies. Here are some others.

Other Misconceptions

The following factors have all been considered part of an
overall business strategy. Some have been used successfully;
others were disastrous. I offer them as a series of do's and
don'ts in developing your strategy. I caution you not to let
these factors distract you from the core concept of strategy.
Here's what we'll be discussing:

- Creativity vs. size
- Needs vs. wants
- A moving target
- Built-in obsolescence
- Wake-up calls
- Mergers & acquisitions
- Industry consolidation

Creativity Matters, Size Doesn't

A 10-person insurance agency gained the lion's share of its
local construction industry market by offering to collect the
certificates of insurance for their customers.

For those of you not familiar with certificates of insurance
here's how they work. Whenever your company hires a
contractor, it has two options with regard to insurance:

1. It can get a certificate from the contractor's insurance company showing that the contractor carries liability and workmen's compensation insurance.
2. It can pay additional premiums on its own liability and workmen's compensation policies.

Generally, you prefer to have contractors provide their own insurance coverage. If they do, you must have a certificate on file showing that the contractor has the required coverage; otherwise, your company incurs additional premiums. Ouch! These premiums are based on the amounts paid to uninsured contractors (when there's no evidence of coverage) at the rates included in your company's policy. As you might suspect, maintaining an up-to-date certificate file is a hassle.

First, it usually takes several phone calls to get certificates because contractors view them as distractions that take them from their real business.

Second, the policies come due at different times during the year. That means you need a tracking system to assure that the certificates you have are current.

Finally, the people hiring contractors are usually not the ones responsible for the company's insurance programs. It's not unusual for the insurance people to learn about a contractor *after* the project is complete, when it's even more difficult to get a certificate. As you can see, certificates of insurance are an administrative nightmare.

By taking responsibility for collecting these certificates, this agency provides a unique service that offers real value to its customers. In return, it gains several benefits.

First, the agency's customers are more loyal because an administrative headache has been eliminated. Second, price sensitivity declines; the agency's customers are willing to pay a little more to avoid dealing with these certificates. Finally, this agency learns about new contractors *as soon as they appear on the scene.* What a marketing opportunity! I love strategies with multiple benefits, don't you?

There are larger agencies in this market, but this agency beat its larger competitors by offering a unique service. Creativity matters; size doesn't. Talk to your customers and prospects. Find out what they want or need. Provide it. Then enjoy the ride as you take market share from your larger competitors.

> *Creativity matters; size doesn't.*
> *Your company can compete with larger firms.*

Our next section, *Needs vs. Wants,* recognizes that buyers have different attitudes towards what they want and what they need.

Needs vs. Wants

Many companies focus on their customers' needs. That's a viable strategy, but the greatest profit potential exists in providing what they *want*. Doubt that? Take a look at the big accounting firms and their revenue mix during the early years of their movement into consulting services.

In the six years from 1993 through 1998, the top 5 firms[3] experienced the following revenue mix:

---

[3] The top five firms in 1998 were actually six in 1993; a merger reduced their number. The revenue data includes the same firms for both years. The five became four in 2003 as Arthur Anderson fell as a result of its contribution to the Enron fiasco.

	Consulting revenues	Traditional CPA revenues
1998	$12.3 billion[4]	$14.0 billion
1993	$ 3.5 billion	$ 8.7 billion
percentage increase	251%	61%

Figure 1.1 below, shows the disparity in revenue growth rates. Let's explore the reasons behind this disparity.

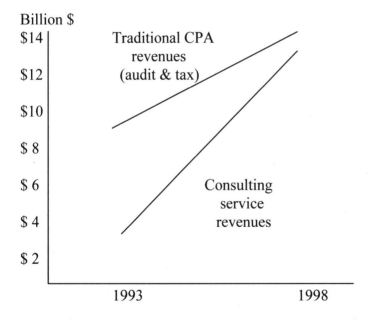

Figure 1.1 Comparison of growth rates of traditional CPA services vs. Consulting services 1993-1998

---

[4]   A special thanks to John McKenna at Strafford Publications, Inc.'s "Public Accounting Report," Atlanta, GA, for gathering this data.

Consulting clients *want* help increasing shareholder returns. Their jobs depend on it. That's why they're willing to pay handsomely for advice that will help them achieve that goal.

Audit and tax work are considered necessary evils. These services don't:

- increase shareholder value; although they might preserve it
- advance managers' careers
- enhance managers' financial success

When viewed from this perspective, is it any wonder that management wants to pay as little as possible for these services? What's the moral of this story?

> ***When offered a choice between serving your customers' wants or their needs, serve their wants; it pays better.***

Sounds simple, right? It would be if customers' desires weren't continually changing.

A Moving Target

One of the most common mistakes companies make is staying with a strategy after the market moves on. It's easy to do. When things are going well, you feel that you've got it all figured out. You become complacent and stop monitoring your markets.

When the first sales decline hits, you attribute it to a soft economy or some other innocuous condition. You're in denial. The denial continues until the need for action becomes obvious. Hopefully, you haven't waited so long that survival is an issue. Does any of this sound familiar?

How do you avoid this mistake? Constantly monitor your markets; anticipate their needs/wants. How? Place yourself in the customer's shoes; ask:

- What's disappointing about this product/service?
- What could this product/service be doing to make my life easier?
- How will this product/service help me meet my customers' desires in the next two to three years?

If you can't come up with the answers to these questions, it's imperative that you:

- Visit your customers and ask them the same questions
- Observe your customers using your products/services
- Ask customers to evaluate various aspects of your offerings *and* your competitors' offerings
- Visit your competitors' customers; learn why they're unwilling to change vendors; ask what their needs/ wants are going to be in the next 2 to 3 years

Even if you can answer the first set of questions above, it's worthwhile to validate your answers using the second group of questions. That's how you enable yourself to consistently hit a moving target.

Customer wants/needs are continually changing. In order to be successful, your company must learn to consistently hit this moving target.

Tremendous rewards await companies that develop this skill. These companies enjoy higher profits because there is little, if any, competition. The lack of competition allows them to build higher than usual margins into their pricing and get it.

The cash generated by these higher margins can be used to widen the lead over competitors. How? The title of the next section should give you a clue.

Built-in Obsolescence

Don't be afraid to make your products or services obsolete. Some of the most successful companies in the world have used this strategy to their advantage.

Intel and Hewlett-Packard's printer division are both known for their ability to keep competitors scrambling to catch up. Just as their competitors begin to close the gap, Intel and HP make their offerings (and those their competitors are about to launch) obsolete. Here's a more complete description of how it works.

Let's say that your company provides something the market wants that it currently isn't getting. Since your company is the only one offering this product/service, it gets higher than usual prices and profit margins.

Your competitors scramble to catch up. Just as they are about to introduce their versions of your offering, you reduce your price. Ouch!

They probably invested as much as you did in developing the offering, but they're going to recover the investment much more slowly. Why? Their profit margins are lower. They aren't going to get the premium pricing and margins you did.

Next, you invest the profit advantage you gained in another product/service that satisfies a customer want and repeat the cycle. It doesn't take much imagination to experience how frustrating the game of catch-up can be.

The only way a competitor can break this cycle is to leapfrog you. They need to offer something the market wants that you aren't providing. Usually, this happens when your company gets comfortable with its position in the industry. We see this all the time in sports.

Think of one of your favorite sports teams. Remember a time when they used an aggressive offensive strategy to develop a commanding lead. What happened when they switched to defense, to *protecting* their lead? The lead evaporated, didn't it? The same holds true in business.

When a company gets comfortable with its position, when it stops putting pressure on its competitors, it opens a passing lane for its competitors to race by. When that happens, roles reverse and the previous leader finds itself having to invest heavily to regain its lead.

Make your company's offerings obsolete before your competitors do. It's financially rewarding and a lot more fun than playing catch up.

Even when you do all the things we've just discussed, you're creative, you sell wants rather than needs, you consistently satisfy your customers' needs and you build obsolescence into your offerings, you will face factors outside your control.

Wake-up Calls
Occasionally you'll be reminded that you're not completely in control of your company's destiny. Even a well-designed

strategy and persistent attention to detail, can't protect your
business from getting clobbered with the proverbial 2 by 4.

Intel's CEO, Andy Grove, calls these sudden changes in the
fundamentals of your business "strategic inflection points"[5].
According to Mr. Grove, strategic inflection points can either
be an opportunity to rise to new heights or the signal for the
beginning of the end.

Strategic inflection points are major shifts in how markets
will be served in the future, if they exist at all. Usually these
shifts are unexpected and well outside the realm of "normal
evolution" of product/service improvements. These shifts
often punctuate the fact that the market wants/needs weren't
being met. How else can we explain such dramatic and
traumatic change?

Examples
In the 1970s, Japan's auto industry gave a wake-up call to
U.S. automakers by dramatically improving quality. Japan
recognized what the Big Three did not; U.S. auto buyers were
fed up with cars that required thousands of dollars of repairs
as soon as they hit the 50,000-mile mark. As long as there
wasn't any competition, the U.S. automakers didn't feel the
need to change their strategy. Japan's entry into the U.S.
market became a strategic inflection point.

The Clinton administration's healthcare initiative created a
strategic inflection point for PSS/World Medical, Inc. This
initiative put pressure on all healthcare providers to cut costs.
In response to this pressure PSS customers shifted their focus
from superior service to low prices. Did that shift give PSS

---

[5]Andrew S. Grove, *Only the Paranoid Survive*, Doubleday, October 1996

license to abandon its service strategy? Of course not! Their customers had become accustomed to exceptional service; they weren't about to go back. Would you?

PSS had the daunting task of cutting costs *without* reducing service and they answered the challenge admirably. I won't steal Mr. Kelly's thunder. If you're interested in learning how his team managed this transition, the answer lies in Mr. Kelly's book, *Faster Company.*

These are only two examples of strategic inflection points. On any given day your business could face new regulations, industry deregulation, new environmental concerns, new technologies and new competitors. Each of these has the potential to change the fundamentals of your business.

Andy Grove's book, *Only the Paranoid Survive*, provides tools for identifying and using strategic inflection points to create a stronger, healthier company. It is an insightful, easy read with powerful messages.

Wake-up calls are stressful times in an organization's life. Organizations that are creative and possess mental toughness thrive; for the others, survival is questionable.

One of the ways that organizations adapt to an ever-changing world is through mergers and acquisitions. How effective are they? Let's take a look.

Mergers and Acquisitions

There are many reasons why two companies merge, but the real question is, "Can we predict which ones will succeed and which will not?"

The key to a successful merger is the same as for a successful business strategy, to provide the market with something it wants or needs that it currently isn't getting. To help us understand this premise, let's look at some mergers.

The Cisco Experience
During the years 1994 through 1999, Cisco Systems successfully completed 42 acquisitions.[6] Why were they so successful? Two reasons:

1. Their acquisitions brought them new and developing technologies to enhance their existing offerings.
2. They assimilated their processes into the acquired company without stifling employee creativity.

New technologies
I'm sure some of you are wondering, "If Cisco acquired technology that already existed, how could the merger have qualified as providing something the market wanted that it wasn't getting?" Good question. Cisco wasn't providing new technology; it was providing *awareness* of the new technology. Cisco recognized three market realities:

1. There are so many companies developing new technologies that it's virtually impossible for the business community to know what's available.
2. Many companies involved in developing technology don't have the marketing budgets to reach their potential customers.
3. Even if a fledgling technology company did have a large marketing budget, it would take years for it to gain the kind of brand awareness Cisco has.

---

[6] Fortune Magazine, November 8, 1999, Volume 140 #9 page 177, Cisco's Secrets by Henry Goldblatt

By purchasing new technologies, Cisco offered its customers the latest innovations with the assurance of Cisco quality and the speed of Cisco's distribution systems. That's one-half of the equation; the other relates to employee assimilation.

Assimilating employees and systems
Cisco also took great pains to assimilate the workforces of each of the acquired companies. As you'll see in Chapter 8, *Work Environment*, employees' attitudes have a tremendous impact on your customers' experience.

Cisco invested heavily in easing the transition for employees of newly-acquired companies. They wanted these workers to feel like a valued member of the Cisco family. They also wanted these new employees to retain much of the autonomy they had before the acquisition. Cisco's leadership knew that creativity would suffer if autonomy was lost. Cisco wasn't just buying new technology, it was buying future innovation.

The customer focus in Cisco's acquisition strategy and its attention to workers' needs combined to make Cisco one of the most successful acquirers in merger/acquisition history.

Unfortunately, not all mergers are so successful. Let's look at a merger that hasn't lived up to expectations.

DaimlerChrysler
In November 1998 Daimler and Chrysler merged to the considerable pleasure of Wall Street. The succeeding five years' earnings have disappointed everyone, management, the financial community and stockholders alike.

There were two strong indicators that this deal would not work quite as well as the financial community envisioned. First, analysts at the major brokerage houses touted the potential cost savings to both companies. Second, they didn't mention what the newly-formed company was going to offer customers that they couldn't already get.

Cutting costs

If cost-cutting was the primary motive for this merger, it was destined for trouble from the first day it was conceived. That may sound harsh, but the reality is that the benefits of cost-cutting are short-lived. Why?

As human beings we're creatures of habit. It's natural for us to use approaches that have served us well in the past. That's why employees, once they become comfortable in their new jobs, return to old habits including the way in which they manage their budgets. The fact that the employee survived the merger affirms that their earlier approaches were correct, so why not employ them again. With that psychology at work, is it any wonder that mergers based on cost-cutting usually produce disappointing results?

I'm not the only one with this opinion. Dr. Fritz Kroeger of A. T. Kearney, a global consulting firm, says that the third deadly sin of mergers is "focusing on cost-cutting rather than growth." He goes on to say, "growth is the byproduct of competitive advantage – that requires a unique offering."

The second indicator that the DaimlerChrysler merger was going to be disappointing is that it didn't offer anything *new* to the customers these two companies served. In fact, these companies serve two very different markets.

No unique offering
Daimler customers buy prestige and superb quality in a very
recognizable automobile line. Chrysler's customers delight in
unique, continuously-changing styles. They tolerate below-
average quality to get eye-catching designs at an affordable
price. So what does this merger really do?

It gives Daimler a wider array of markets to serve, but what
do the customers gain? In the long run Daimler may benefit
from Chrysler's ability to create new designs quickly, but
Daimler doesn't change designs all that often. The merger
may help Chrysler improve its quality. Even if it does, it
takes years for customers to recognize quality improvements.

So far, neither Daimler's nor Chrysler's customers have seen
any significant advantages from the merger. That's why the
results have been so lackluster. Time will tell whether this
situation can be remedied.

The Hewlett Packard and Compaq merger may be facing the
same challenges that DaimlerChrysler is. It's another merger
that seems to offer limited customer benefits.

Hewlett Packard/Compaq
This merger is especially intriguing because of the well-
publicized stockholder fight. The fight revolved around the
question of whether this merger was the right strategic move
for Hewlett Packard (HP).

What does HP hope to gain from this merger? One of the
things they hope to do is compete more effectively in the
global server market. Certainly, this is an area in which HP
was deficient, but, according to the financial press, Compaq

hasn't been faring all that well either. How does merging these two companies solve this problem?

As I try to understand this merger, I keep coming back to the same questions, "What do customers gain? What will they get that they couldn't get before?" I don't see anything.

If I'm mistaken, if the new HP is offering something truly unique, why haven't we heard about it? Why haven't we seen press releases or ads clearly communicating these advantages? Why, more than a year after the merger, are we hearing product announcements about imaging devices, HP's strength, rather than increased server capabilities?

I suspect the reason is that the new HP doesn't have a clearly unique server offering to tout. If it did, I'm confident this premier marketing organization would have let us know.

While I don't believe that the new HP will run into financial difficulty as a result of this merger, I doubt that there will be any significant return on their Compaq investment until they find a unique capability that the market values.

By the way, cost reduction was also highly touted in the Hewlett Packard/Compaq merger. I won't belabor the point; you already know my views on using mergers to cut costs.

Mergers and acquisitions are most successful
when they create new ways to serve the customer.

Mergers are often used in industry consolidations. Some say that the reason behind these mergers is cost-cutting. Is that true? Let's take a look.

Industry Consolidation

Some industries have more sellers than buyers. This could occur because:

1. demand for the industry's offerings is waning
2. too many companies have entered a hot market
3. companies in the industry overestimated demand and overbuilt capacity

Whatever the reason, product/service availability exceeds customers' demands. In situations like this, the market is served well by industry consolidation, by stronger companies acquiring or driving out of business weaker competitors.

While many of us bristle at the thought of these painful times, the reality is that virtually all industries experience the need for consolidation at some point in their existence. Why? The normal product/profit margin life cycle shown in Figure 1.2 will help answer that question.

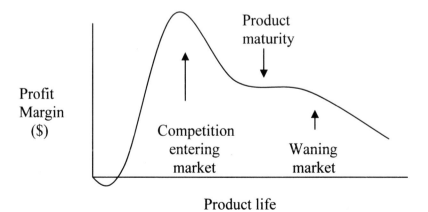

Figure 1.2 Product/profit margin life cycle

In the very early stage of the product's life, profit dollars are negative (a loss); that's because the initial capacity exceeds demand for the product. As demand rises, profit dollars rise dramatically. Why? There is little, if any, competition for the company introducing the product. Lack of competition allows that company to get a premium price for its offering, which means that it is typically enjoying higher than usual profit margins.

As competitors see the profit potential of the new offering, they develop competing offerings. It's during this phase of a product's life that excess capacity is often created. That usually triggers the first round of industry consolidation. The purpose of consolidation is to bring supply and demand back into alignment. Cost reduction is a byproduct, not a goal of industry consolidation.

After consolidation, profit margins return to a level that's typical for the industry. Those profits continue until one of two things happen:

1. a new product/service is developed to replace the existing offering
2. the market becomes saturated (the market for VHS recorders became saturated even before the advent of DVD technology)

Both of these conditions are capable of triggering another round of industry consolidation.

The most successful companies replace their products/ services *before* their competitors do. We discussed that concept in the *Built-in Obsolescence* section above.

Other well-managed companies opt out of a market as margins drop below a certain level. They choose to move onto more fertile fields.

Unfortunately, some companies continue to fight a losing battle. Their managers are in denial; management's failure to confront harsh realities raises serious questions about the company's survival. The choice is yours, which of these approaches would you like to see your company adopt?

Industry consolidations are inevitable.
Make sure that your strategy includes a plan
for dealing with them.

We've covered a lot of ground in this opening chapter. It's not my intent to overwhelm you, but to provide a broad overview of the issues involved in business strategy. Even if you're not yet in a position to influence strategy, you need to know what your company's strategy is. You and your staff's performance depend heavily on your ability to align your department's efforts to the company's strategy.

Before we move onto Chapter 2, *Marketing*, let's take a moment to review the core concept of business strategy.

Core Concept – Business Strategy

The key to every successful business strategy is to provide the market with something it wants or needs that it isn't getting.

Executive Summary – Business Strategy

- If your company doesn't have a unique offering, buyers have no reason to buy from you.

- Companies that use price to differentiate themselves from their competitors often run into problems as they grow because they don't control their overhead costs.

- Only companies with a passion for accomplishing more with less should consider a low-price strategy.

- Given a choice between selling what your customers want or what they need, sell what they want; it pays better.

- Customers' wants/needs are a moving target. Unless you're close to your customers, you won't know how those wants/needs are changing.

- Make your offerings obsolete before your competitors do.

- Sometimes, despite doing everything right, factors outside your control will render your strategy worthless. You can bemoan the situation or view it as a test of your company's resilience and creativity.

- Mergers and acquisitions should create a competitive advantage. They're not useful in cutting costs.

- Industry consolidations are inevitable and usually come in two waves. The first occurs during the early years as the industry expands quickly in response to a rapidly growing market. The second occurs when demand for a product wanes. Anticipate these consolidations in your strategy.

MARKETING:

How would you characterize your marketing message?

Headline, obituary or somewhere in between?

2

Marketing

What is the goal of every successful marketing effort?

**To create a memory so that buyers think of YOU
when they're ready to buy.**

Core concept – Create Memories

It's mid-summer. The temperature is 95 degrees with 85%
humidity and your air conditioner just shot craps. Can you
name a reputable contractor? No? Then the contractors in
your area haven't done a very good job of marketing their
services, have they? How does this affect you?

You have to scour the Yellow Pages for contractors, contact the Better Business Bureau on the two or three in your area; then call each of them to check their availability and pricing. That's a lot of work and a terrible waste of your time.

Now, let's contrast that with what happens when a local contractor creates a *memorable* marketing message. You know which brands of air conditioners he services, what his normal response time is, how long he's been in business and that he hasn't had a claim filed with the Better Business Bureau since he's been in business.

You'll still make the call to the Better Business Bureau to verify his claim, but once that's done you'll call him and set the appointment - easy for you, profitable for him.

As we've just seen, memorable marketing messages have the potential to increase sales *and* enhance your customer's experience. I love multiple benefits!

Now that you have a sense for what a memorable marketing message can do, let's see what's required to create one. Here are four elements to consider when crafting or revamping your marketing message:

1. Universal message
2. Humor
3. Pain/dreams
4. Call to action

Before we explore these factors, I want to explain why all the examples in this chapter relate to retail marketing. All of you are retail customers. My guess is that few of you have much business-to-business marketing experience. By using retail examples, I hope to make it easier for you to validate the following messages with your personal experience.

The concepts discussed in this chapter apply equally well to retail and business-to-business marketing. How can I be so sure? People, not companies, make business-to-business buying decisions. Now, let's explore the four elements of a marketing message beginning with the universal message.

Universal Message

If you hope to create a successful marketing message you must know what your customers value. Sounds simple, right? In reality, it is one of the most confounding problems business leaders face. Why? Variety!

Most businesses offer a broad array of products/services to serve an equally diverse group of customers. On top of that, each offering provides multiple benefits. The challenge is to find a universal message, one that speaks to your customers about what they value most. Sound like a daunting task?

It doesn't have to be *if* you realize that your value proposition is the same for all of your offerings. Whether the value you provide is superior quality, low prices, exceptional service or innovation, it should be the same for all of your offerings.

Still not sure what your company's value proposition is? Let's take a look at how one business owner discovered her company's value proposition.

During a presentation to a chamber of commerce, I asked the audience to perform the following tasks within two minutes:

1. Define their market, the universe of people/companies that could use their offerings
2. Identify their customers, those people within the universe they are targeting
3. Differentiate their products/services from their competitors' offerings

At the end of the two minutes I asked three volunteers to share their analysis with the group. One volunteer, a physical therapist, nailed the value proposition. Here's what she said:

> *"As I thought about my customers - athletes with sport injuries, heart attack survivors, stroke victims, elderly people with broken hips and other fall-related injuries - I realized that all my customers want the same thing, <u>to feel better</u>."*

"Feeling better" is her universal message. It's the common thread that ties together everything she does. It's what her customers value.

Once you have the universal message it's easy to tailor that message to any market you serve. How? Let's take a look.

Tailoring the message

You tailor marketing messages by looking at the customer group you're serving (or want to serve) and asking, "What does my universal message mean to them?"

Our physical therapist could ask herself, "What makes athletes feel better?" Athletes feel better when they return to competitive form. Our therapist needs to tailor her message to emphasize how quickly she can help athletes regain that competitive edge.

How would you answer the question, "What makes heart attack victims feel better?" If you said, "Heart attack victims feel better when they can engage in their normal activities without fearing another heart attack." *Voila!* The tailored message paints a picture of a normal life *without* fear of another heart attack.

Similarly, stroke victims and elderly people feel better when they regain mobility and independence. Our therapist's marketing message would show stroke victims and elderly people enjoying the freedom mobility affords us all.

Now that we've gone through this exercise, can you recall the universal messages of these companies?

Company	**Universal message**
Ford	
Miller Brewing	
Martha Stewart	
Wal-Mart	

Any luck? Here are the universal messages:

Ford	Quality is job one
Miller Brewing	Fun
Martha Stewart	Affordable elegance
Wal-Mart	Always low prices

It doesn't matter whether Ford is promoting the Taurus or the Ranger pickup, quality is job one. Miller Brewing says that you're going to have fun whether you're drinking Miller or

Miller Lite. At Wal-Mart you're going to get a low price whether you're buying clothing, cameras or camping gear.

The leaders of these companies know why you're choosing them over their competitors. That's why every marketing piece includes their universal message. That's what makes their marketing so memorable.

Finding the universal message for your company's offerings isn't an option; it's a necessity. Still struggling to find your company's universal message? Try this approach:

1   Identify your market - *List everyone who might use your company's products or services. Don't exclude anyone from the list.*

2   List your top 20 customers – *What do they value in your offerings? Why do they buy from you rather than your competitors? What keeps them from moving their business to a competitor? What values, interests and needs do each of these customers possess? How do the markets that you serve differ from those you're not serving?*

The answers to these questions will help you identify your universal message.

A universal message makes it easy to tailor specific messages to each market your company serves.

Now that you have a message, how do you present it? Should it be serious or humorous? The answer lies in the second element of a marketing message, humor.

Humor

Think about some of your favorite TV commercials. I'll bet they scored high on your laugh meter. Humor is a great way to create memories. Yet, humor can be risky.

First, there are businesses that just don't lend themselves to the use of humor. If you are a mortician, it's going to be tough to develop a humorous message that doesn't offend potential buyers.

Second, few buyers appreciate all humor styles. In fact, virtually everyone finds some humor styles objectionable. Anheuser-Busch's "Wasssup!" commercial won international acclaim, yet I thought it was ridiculous. That's probably because I'm a generation beyond the college crowd, but it's an example of how buyers' views on humor differ.

Finally, humor can overshadow your message. Think about an ad that had you rolling on the floor with laughter. Now ask yourself, "What were they selling?" and "Who was the advertiser?" If you can't answer these questions, the humor overshadowed the message. Remember, the purpose of your marketing message is to create a memory so that buyers think of you when they're ready to buy.

If you are considering humor (I hope you are), I'd suggest that you use focus groups to help you gauge the humor's impact. Focus groups are customers or potential customers assembled to evaluate some aspect of your offering. In this case they'd be evaluating your marketing message.

Humor is a powerful marketing tool, but it is risky.
Humor may be inappropriate for your type of business, it
could offend buyers or it might overshadow your message.

I've been talking a lot about ads in the last few paragraphs because it's easier to demonstrate the concept of humor using ads, particularly television ads. Don't let that dissuade you from using humor in print ads, radio ads, brochures or direct mail pieces. It can work well in all those media.

We've just been faced with a choice, whether or not to use humor. The third element of our marketing message offers another choice, a choice between targeting a customer's pain or his dreams.

Pain/Dreams

Your universal message is in place and humor decision has been made; now it's time to decide whether to focus your message on the buyer's pain or his dreams. These are two dramatically different approaches. Let's explore pain first.

Pain

I'm not talking about creating pain; I'm talking about using the buyer's pain to get him to buy. Pain is effective because people are averse to pain; they want to rid themselves of it as quickly as possible. Pain creates urgency, which makes it an attractive marketing approach.

How do you make the buyer's pain work for you?

- Show the buyer that he's not alone
- Offer hope; your product will alleviate his pain
- Demonstrate success

Not alone

It's important for buyers to realize that they are not alone, that others experience the same pain they do. Isn't it easier for you to discuss a problem you're having after learning that someone else is wrestling the same problem? Sure, it is. We believe that our problems are unique when, in reality, most of us experience very similar problems throughout our lives.

How can you show buyers that others share their pain? You can use statistics, but it's hard for people to commiserate with numbers. Imagine how you would feel if Subway restaurants quoted obesity statistics. "Fifteen percent of the population is at least 20 pounds overweight." Do you feel any connection with this group? Not likely; they're faceless. You can't see them or their pain so how can you possibly connect?

Subway understands this need for personal connection; that's why they got Jared to share his experience. Jared's battle with obesity is something you can relate to even if you're only ten pounds overweight! It's not the amount of weight that creates the connection; it's the struggle to shed excess pounds that forms the bond.

If you want your buyers to realize that they're not alone, use stories of individuals who experienced the same pain.

If we stopped here, if all we did was establish a connection with the pain, we wouldn't get the buyer to act. We need to offer a solution. That brings us to the second component of pain marketing, hope.

Hope

Buyers need hope; otherwise, they have no reason to buy. How's that for stating the obvious?

If that's so obvious, why do advertisers ask you to accept their word that their product/service is going to solve your problem? When I say "accept their word", I mean without demonstrating any tangible result.

Hope is a byproduct of demonstrated results, not cleverly written text. It's Jared's "before" and "after" photos, it's hearing him tell his story of losing 235 pounds that allows others who are fighting obesity, to gain hope. Without these results, Subway's claims would be viewed as pure conjecture. Rightfully so!

Demonstrated results offer buyers their greatest hope.

Demonstrated results, success stories, are essential in offering buyers hope, but not all success stories are equally effective.

Success stories
Once again, we need to explore human nature to understand buyers' reactions to success stories. How do you feel when you hear an extraordinary success story? Do you accept it at face value or do you wonder if there's more to the story?

My guess is that you are skeptical. If so, you have a lot of company. Most of us doubt things that seem too good to be true. That skepticism is part of our defense system; it helps us avoid trouble. It also makes marketers' lives difficult. How do you overcome skepticism?

First, *demonstrate the results; don't just state them.* It's hard evidence, and lots of it, that overcomes skepticism, usually. Why am I hedging? The source of the evidence can also be subject to skepticism.

When you see Ford, General Motors or Honda do their crash tests do you ever wonder whether the test was designed to show the desired result? I'm not suggesting that the people at Ford, GM or Honda are devious; rather I'm saying that buyers distrust claims companies make about their offerings. Why?

Buyers know that it's natural for a company's employees to take pride in the products and services they're offering. This attitude can subconsciously influence test designs so that they produce desired results. I want to emphasize the fact that this often goes on subconsciously. Let's use a personal example to illustrate this point.

Think about a time when someone found an error in a report or presentation you prepared. Were you dismayed that the error existed? Why? You triple checked your work before presenting it. You *believed* it was accurate, yet an error was overlooked. How does this happen?

Subconsciously, you believe your work is correct because you've taken great care in performing the task. As you review your work your eye sees what your mind intended, not what exists. That's how bias develops.

It's the subconscious mind's propensity for bias that makes it easy to construct tests to produce the desired results without being aware that you're doing it. Let me emphasize, again, malicious intent is not needed for test results to be skewed, all that's required is bias. Since companies are run by people, we know that bias exists in every organization.

How can you overcome this bias and the buying public's cynical nature? Use third party testimonials. Notice that I used the plural, testimonials; one success story typically isn't enough to sway a skeptical buyer.

While Jared's success story is amazing, by itself, it may not be enough to overcome your skepticism. By adding more success stories, Subway makes it increasingly difficult for you to doubt the results.

There are times when success stories aren't available, such as when you're launching a new offering. At times like this, you consider independent testing or, if you have a healthy budget, celebrity endorsements.

Ford, GM and Honda gain credibility by using independent authorities like J.D. Powers and Consumer Reports to support their claims. Touting the results of independent testing is a great way to gain consumer confidence, and it's a lot less expensive than celebrity endorsements.

Celebrities can enhance the credibility of success stories, *if* the buying public trusts them. Former U. S. Senator Robert Dole has done ads for both Pfizer and Pepsi. Regardless of whether you agree with his politics, most of you would agree that Mr. Dole has the reputation of being a man of integrity, strong convictions and sound values. These qualities make him a natural as a spokesperson.

Unfortunately, celebrities are as human as the rest of us and they make mistakes too. I'm sure that, with a few moments' reflection, you'll think of two or three celebrity spokespeople who have been charged with criminal acts. The loss of their credibility may not cast a shadow on the offerings they represent, but it certainly won't enhance the offering's image.

If you don't have the kind of budget celebrity endorsements require, third party testimonials from your customers will do very nicely. Remember, it's important that the testimonials *demonstrate*, rather than *state* the results.

When using pain to develop a marketing message, let the buyer know that he's not alone in his suffering, offer him hope, then regale him with success stories.

Pain is an effective approach in marketing, but it isn't the only approach available to you. You can also tap into the buyers' dreams. Let's see how that works.

Dreams

As we've just seen pain is an avoidance strategy; you help the buyer *avoid* pain. Dreams are attraction strategies. By tapping into their dreams, your goal is to *attract* buyers to your offerings. How? By creating desire where it didn't exist or rekindling desire that's dormant.

Let's say that you're watching television when a car with an incredible new design appears. You won't be happy until you get one. Or you've just seen a program demonstrating that new sponge painting technique. You look at your walls and realize that it's time for a change. These ads create a desire for change; that's attraction marketing.

Unfortunately, dreams create little, if any, sense of urgency. Here's the problem. Dreams appeal to the child in us. As adults, we suppress the child and persuade ourselves to do the "responsible thing." That means putting our dreams on hold. When that happens, dreams become disappointments. That's not what dream marketing is intended to do. How can you avoid this problem? Anticipate the adult response.

Dream marketing should raise and answer questions about what might keep the buyer from buying. If you're Miller Lite or Michelob, realize that many buyers don't believe that they have time to host a party. Show them how to throw parties that don't require a lot of work. Have a maid service get the house ready. Show each guest bringing a dish. Better yet, open snacks, pop the tab and let the party begin. The key to dream marketing is anticipating the buyers' resistance.

If you're Mitsubishi and you're introducing a new sports car, show buyers how to minimize their payments. Show them how to roll their existing financing into their new loan; that makes trading early affordable. Help buyers deal with their adult responsibilities so that they can enjoy the toy they want.

Dreams can be powerful motivators; unfortunately, too many of us have grown accustomed to foregoing dreams for the "realities" of life. That's a shame. That also makes your life as a marketer more challenging. If you're going to use dreams as a marketing strategy, be prepared to anticipate and eliminate resistance.

Dreams usually don't create a sense of urgency for the buyer. To instill urgency, show the buyer how to indulge the child within him while acting responsibly.

We've covered the first three elements of a memorable marketing message, the universal message, humor and pain/dreams. Let's turn to our fourth and final element, the call to action.

Call to Action

Every marketing message needs a call to action. You cannot trust buyers to act on their own. In today's fast-paced world it's easy for buyers to dismiss pain as "not that bad," even easier to postpone dreams. That's why marketing messages need a call to action.

Retailers are very good at this. Their ads say "this weekend only," "from 7:00 a.m. to 9:00 a.m," "while supply lasts." Time limits are one of the most effective calls to action. So is supply. Don't be fooled into thinking that we're talking only about product sales now. Concerts and seminars use limited seating as a way to get buyers to register early.

The key to creating a call to action is to limit some aspect of the offering. Buyers are more likely to act when they feel that failing to do so will result in a lost opportunity. This may seem counterintuitive, but the reality is that more sales are lost to buyer inaction than to limitations on the offering. That's right; more sales are lost because buyers don't have a sense of urgency than because the offer is limited. Doubt that? See if either of these situations sound familiar?

You just saw an ad for a fly rod made of a new composite that allows you to feel even the lightest strike. Or the ad announces that the latest fall fashions have arrived. Neither ad suggests the items are on sale or indicates that supplies are limited. How quickly are you going to act?

Unless you were already planning to go to that store, you'll probably make a note to check that rod or those fashions the next time you're there. When will that be? Tomorrow? Next week? Next month? Will you remember to check on those items when you're there?

Let's be honest. If we don't act on something immediately, the likelihood of forgetting about it rises exponentially with the passage of time. That's why I say that more sales are lost to buyer inaction than to limitations on the offerings. Don't let that happen to you; create a call to action.

EVERY marketing message needs a call to action; often that involves limiting some aspect of your offering.

There you have it, the four elements for creating memorable marketing messages:

1.   Universal message
2.   Humor
3.   Pain/Dreams
4.   Call to action

Now that we have our marketing message, let's explore some other marketing misconceptions.

Other Misconceptions

One of the best marketing books I've ever read is *Guerilla Marketing.*[7] The author, Jay Conrad Levinson, dispelled a lot of myths for me. Here are three valuable insights I gained from his book:

1.   Frequency is more important than perfection in marketing messages.
2.   Marketing doesn't have to be expensive.
3.   For 86% of the population, price is NOT the most important factor in the buying decision.

---

[7] Jay Conrad Levinson, *Guerilla Marketing*, Houghton Mifflin 1984

Let's look at each of these concepts more carefully.

Frequency vs. Perfection

When it comes to marketing messages, one of the greatest challenges you'll face is ending the process. You're never quite satisfied with the message so you keep tweaking it.

Every day that you spend working on your message costs you money. Why? Studies show that buyers must see or hear your message *more than two dozen times before they buy*. Can you imagine how long it takes to make twenty four contacts *without* antagonizing the buyer?

Besides, how many details do you remember from marketing messages you hear? Let's be honest. When you're tweaking your message, you're working on details. Is that really what you want buyers to remember? Of course not! You want them to recall the universal message, not the details. Let's stop this lunacy. Set a deadline for completing your message. Then repeat it often.

What's often? It depends on the type of business you have. Retailers should be contacting their buyers at least once a week. For other businesses, monthly may be adequate. I can't think of a business in which the frequency should drop below once a month.

Remember, the goal of marketing is to have buyers think of you when they're ready to buy. Out of sight, out of mind is an apt description of what happens if buyers don't hear your name at least once a month. Remember:

Frequency is more important than perfection
in marketing messages.

Owners and managers of smaller businesses often think that marketing is easier for large corporations because they have huge advertising budgets. Marketing is more than running ads; it's *any* activity that places your name and universal message in front of potential buyers. That brings us to the second insight gleaned from *Guerilla Marketing*; marketing need not be expensive.

Expensive

Money is currency, but so are time and good deeds. If you don't have the money for advertising, direct mail or similar marketing efforts, donate time to a local charity, a school or support a local relief effort. It's a great way to get publicity for your company without the cost of a public relations firm.

I know that I've just invited the public relations profession to inundate me with letters. Let me assure all of you in public relations that I appreciate the value you provide, but let's be honest. It doesn't make sense for a company that has more time than money to avail itself of your services. Certainly you have the skill to help these firms, but their budgetary constraints will limit your effectiveness. You're better off working with firms that have more money than time.

Another way to keep marketing costs down is to piggyback onto another firm's marketing efforts. Offer them, or their customers, a discount on your products/services. Your partners get an opportunity to make more money and build customer loyalty. Their customers/prospects can save money on your offerings. You reach new markets for your offerings. It's the classic "win-win".

These are just a couple of ways to market inexpensively. If you want more, I refer you to *Guerilla Marketing*; I couldn't begin to improve on Mr. Levinson's ideas.

> ***Good deeds and piggybacking onto other firms' marketing are two ways of keeping your marketing costs low.***

So far, we've learned that frequency is more important than perfection and marketing need not be expensive. It's time to explore Mr. Levinson's third insight, it's not the price.

It's Not the Price

So many marketing messages focus on low prices that buyers rarely hear what distinguishes one seller from another. You and I both know that sellers' offerings can differ dramatically in quality, service and convenience. Mr. Levinson tells us that these and other factors are more important than price to *86%* of the buying public. What implications does this have for your marketing messages?

If your company is unique in the quality, convenience or service it offers, say so in your marketing messages. Don't bore buyers with price talk when they're not even sure that your product/service will benefit them. As we discussed in *Universal Message* above, tell them about the things they value. Lead with your strengths, not with your price; unless you're Wal-Mart and price is your strength.

> ***Eighty-six percent of the buying public says that price isn't even in the top five considerations when making their buying decisions.***

Mr. Levinson provided us with three valuable insights:

1.   Frequency is more important than a perfect message.
2.   Marketing need not be expensive.
3.   Price is not a major factor in most buying decisions.

All three rectify some long-standing misconceptions about marketing. Here's another one; marketing should be directed toward your customers. What if your customer isn't the end user? Where do you direct your marketing message?

Market to Your Customers' Customer

Shortly after its launch in 1981, NutraSweet arranged to have its customers put the NutraSweet logo on their products. This strategy offered several significant benefits:

1. NutraSweet's customers were able to demonstrate concern for their customers' health; at the time, the level of sugar consumption in the United States was generating health concerns.
2. Companies that included the NutraSweet logo on their products were able to differentiate their offerings from their competitors' offerings.
3. NutraSweet dramatically increased the frequency of its message to the buying public; millions of soft drink cans included the NutraSweet logo.
4. The buying public asked manufacturers of products containing sugar to provide a NutraSweet alternative, further increasing the demand for NutraSweet.

Can you think of other companies that have employed this marketing strategy? The "Intel Inside" campaign comes to mind. Again, by placing their logo on their customers' computer, Intel was able to increase demand for its chips.

Many pharmaceutical companies have recently adopted this strategy. They're running ads touting medications designed to reduce cholesterol, alleviate depression or improve your sex life. The ads, which run on television, are directed at the end user.

Instead of trying to convince doctors to recommend their products, pharmaceutical companies are getting the buying public to ask their doctors whether these medications are right for them. These companies are creating demand by making the ultimate user aware of their product's existence. It's a powerful strategy that isn't employed often enough.

Marketing to your customer's customer is an excellent way of creating demand for your offerings.

Mr. Levinson's insights and marketing to your customer's customer are designed to enhance the effectiveness of your company's marketing efforts. Remember, they are to be considered only in light of the core concept of marketing. What was that concept again?

Core Concept – Marketing

The goal of every successful marketing effort is to create a memory so that buyers think of YOU when they are ready to buy.

Executive Summary – Marketing

- To make a marketing message memorable:

  1. Identify the universal message for your offerings; use that theme to tailor your message to the various markets you serve.
  2. Use humor when possible; use focus groups to assure the humor is appropriate for your target market.
  3. Decide whether to target the customer's pain or dreams.
  4. Include a call to action.

- Pain generally creates greater urgency than dreams.

- Truths gained from the book, *Guerilla Marketing*:

  1. Frequency of contact is more important than a perfect marketing message.
  2. Marketing doesn't have to be expensive.
  3. Eighty-six percent of the buying public says that price isn't even in the top five of consideration in making their buying decisions.

- Whenever possible, market to customers' customers.

When done well, marketing lays the groundwork for your sales force. It gives the buying public information about your company's offerings making it easier for your salespeople to make the sale. That's the next step in the process and the focus of Chapter 3, *Selling*.

SELLING:

What do you feel when you see your competitors talking to your customers?

Panic

OR

Confidence tinged with healthy discomfort?

3

Selling

What is the key to every successful sales effort?

To build rapport with the buyer that's so strong your competitors have a difficult time getting in the door.

Core Concept – Building Rapport

When my wife and I decided to buy our first pickup truck, we didn't have a clue what size truck we needed. All we knew was that we wanted to tow a 5,000 pound camping trailer.

Fortunately, the salesperson at the first dealership was very knowledgeable. He not only understood things like gross vehicle weight, hauling capacity and towing capacity; he could explain them in layman's language. He educated us on the advantages and disadvantages of different gear ratios, suspension systems and cooling systems. The knowledge he shared demonstrated that he was genuinely interested in helping us make an informed decision.

We visited other dealerships. All of the salespeople asked why we wanted a pickup truck then suggested what they felt would meet our needs. A couple of their suggestions didn't make sense in light of the information the first salesperson had given us.

Where did we go when we were ready to buy? To the first salesperson we met, of course. Why? He demonstrated concern for us by taking the time to *educate* us. He built a rapport with us that made it difficult for his competitors to get in the door.

Some of you are probably thinking, "The rapport didn't keep you from visiting other dealerships." You're right. It didn't keep us from shopping and it shouldn't! One of the great misconceptions about selling is that once the buyer walks out the door the sale is lost. That's not true; buyers need to shop. Here's why.

The Need To Shop

Shopping is the mechanism that allows us to feel comfortable with our buying decisions. It allows us to gather information, explore alternatives and make price/value comparisons.

Shopping helps us gain the knowledge we need to make informed decisions. With knowledge comes comfort; that's why shopping, especially for big-ticket items, is so vital to a good buying experience.

Successful salespeople understand these needs and respond to them using a three-step process. They:

1. Help buyers clarify their wants/needs
2. Educate buyers about the options available to them
3. Refer buyers to other sources if their offerings don't meet the buyer's needs; that leaves the door open to future sales

If you've ever dealt with a salesperson that has used this approach, you're sporting a smile right now. How do you feel when a salesperson tries to convince you that you don't need to shop any more? Is that smile still there? Of course not! A stranger is asking you to *believe* that she knows exactly what you need, that her offering is the best value available and that she has your best interests at heart.

Even if the first two are true, she knows what you need and her offering is the best value for you, her actions don't demonstrate that she has your best interests at heart. Why? She's ignoring a need that's very important to you, the need to feel comfortable with your decision. Salespeople who ignore this need often elicit buyer distrust and open the door to their competitors.

Want to avoid this pitfall? Follow the three steps already mentioned above:

1. Help buyers clarify their wants/needs
2. Educate buyers about the options available to them
3. Refer buyers to other sources if their offerings don't meet the buyer's needs

You'll make it difficult for your competitors to get in the door, even though the buyer continues shopping.

In my opening example, the pickup truck salesperson knew that we were going to shop the purchase; we told him that when we walked in the door. He also knew that if he helped us make an informed decision, it would be difficult for his competitors to make the sale in his absence. That's what I mean by making it "difficult for your competitors to get in the door."

Shopping is the mechanism which allows buyers to feel comfortable with their buying decisions. Asking them to forego shopping opens the door for your competitors.

In the next section, we'll explore other aspects of rapport and the benefits it affords.

Rapport

Random House defines rapport as a harmonious relation with another person. All of us have experienced rapport to some degree. Sometimes we call it "chemistry." We're not sure what's in the mix, but we know it's working.

Salespeople can't rely on the randomness of chemistry if they hope to be successful. Instead, they need to learn how to build rapport quickly and do it consciously.

What are the key elements of rapport? How do you establish it? What's involved in strengthening rapport? How is it lost? Let's explore each of these questions.

Key elements of rapport
There are six keys to building rapport over which you have *complete* control:

1. Genuine concern for others
2. Understanding others' needs
3. Respect
4. Integrity
5. Self-respect
6. Consistency

Genuine concern for others
How do you know when someone really cares about you, not romantically, but as a fellow human being? Is it enough that they tell you that they care about you or do you look for something more? Many of us require more than words; we need others to *demonstrate* concern for us.

Salespeople need to *show* buyers that they care. How do they do that? They place buyers needs ahead of theirs; they:

1. Stop worrying about the sale; they employ the three-step process described earlier which allows them to sell more than they ever dreamed possible
2. Focus on helping buyers make informed decisions
3. Are patient and encouraging while educating buyers
4. Help buyers see the advantages and disadvantages of each option available to them
5. Refer buyers to other sources when their offerings doesn't meet buyers' needs

That's how they demonstrate concern for the buyer. That's how they gain their trust. That's how they build rapport. In the process, they give buyers reasons to care about them, to

buy from them. Does that sound like a harmonious relation
to you? It does to me.

> *Place buyers' needs ahead of your own and you'll gain
> their trust and, more often than not, the sale.*

One final note; if you feign concern, buyers will know it.
Your body will betray you. Body language communicates
incongruities between words and intent. Adults intuitively
read body language and, more often than not, correctly
ascertain who's telling the truth and who's fudging. The
odds of successfully faking concern are low. Be genuine in
your concern. It's easier and infinitely more successful.

Concern for others is the first element of building rapport, but
it's not enough. It doesn't do us much good to care about
others if we don't know how we can help them. To do that,
we need to understand their needs.

Understanding others' needs
This goes beyond the realm of helping buyers understand
how your offering is going to satisfy their needs. Actually,
that's the easy part. What's difficult is identifying their
emotional needs and satisfying those as well.

For some buyers it's important to control the situation; they
aren't comfortable unless they feel that they're in control.
Other buyers gain comfort by getting to know the salesperson
before getting down to business. A third group gains comfort
by thoroughly researching the product/service they intend to
purchase. They also need time to assimilate the information
they get. The fourth group is extremely cautious; they have
difficulty making decisions. These buyers require a lot of
time to make a decision. Rush them and you'll lose the sale.

None of these buying styles is inherently good or bad; they are simply realities about the way we're built. Learn to recognize each type of buyer. Understand their emotional needs. Find ways to satisfy those needs. How?

Fortunately, there are excellent behavioral profiling tools available to help you identify, understand and adapt to the needs of each of these groups. Two companies that provide these tools are Profiles International based in Texas and TTI Performance Systems, Ltd., in Arizona. Both companies have designed their tools with the layman in mind.

Understanding the emotional needs of the buyer is as important as understanding their product/service needs.

Two hurdles crossed, four to go. Let's explore the third element of rapport, respect.

Respect
Think of an arrogant person, someone who believes she is superior to others. Would you go out of your way to help her? Could you place her interests ahead of yours? If so, how difficult would it be?

That's how we, as buyers, react to salespeople who exhibit the "expert" mentality. Salespeople with this attitude are, in effect, telling buyers that they aren't smart enough to make their own decisions. That attitude can be exhibited in a variety of ways; here are two of them.

I met with a new client on the same day that he met with his Certified Public Accountant (CPA). When I arrived he told me that his CPA had just blasted him for letting his overhead get out of control.

I'm a CPA and, at that time, I was performing traditional CPA services for other clients. I asked him whether his accountant had offered any suggestions on how to correct the situation. He thought for a moment and said, "No, he just blasted me!"

When I walked out of that meeting I had a new client for my CPA services. How did that happen? My predecessor demeaned our mutual client. He criticized him, but didn't offer any advice. He didn't show the client respect and it cost him the account.

A few months later, this same client said "Dale, regardless of what I ask, you never make me feel stupid." Apparently my predecessor had made him feel stupid; otherwise, he'd have no basis for this observation.

If you want to develop rapport with buyers, respect them.

We've discussed three elements of rapport: concern for buyers, understanding their needs and respect. The fourth element is integrity; let's see how it influences rapport.

Integrity
This one's easy. People who try to deceive you obviously don't care about you. They aren't concerned about your welfare, your emotional needs nor do they respect you.

Lack of integrity goes beyond deceit. Failing to honor your promises, guessing at answers to buyers' questions and side-stepping uncomfortable issues, all raise doubts in the buyers' minds about your integrity. Incongruity between actions and words also indicates a lack of integrity. Give buyers a reason to question your integrity and you invite your competitors to the table.

> **It's virtually impossible to develop rapport with someone who doesn't trust you.**

Earlier we spoke of respect as a key element of rapport. Self-respect is equally important. My definition of self-respect may surprise you.

Self-respect

Respect is a two-way street. While it's important for you to respect buyers, it's equally important that buyers respect you.

Often salespeople credit buyers with more power than they possess. The result is that buyers sense an advantage and act on that advantage to the salesperson's detriment. Fortunately others can't take advantage of you unless you allow it. If you doubt that, here's an example that may convince you that you have more power than you realize.

A few years ago, I was referred into a business whose owners I knew only by reputation. Based on their reputation, I really didn't want to work with them. The problem was that the referral source had referred several other very good clients to me and I didn't feel that I could cherry-pick the referrals. Reluctantly, I accepted them as a client.

Upon receipt of my first invoice, one of the owners called and requested a more detailed invoice. I promised to send a new invoice. He said, "I think it would be more professional, don't you?" I wondered why he wanted me to say that my invoice wasn't professional, but rather than debate the issue I assured him that I would send a more detailed invoice. Again he said, "I think it would be more professional, don't you?" At this point I said, "You've asked for a more detailed invoice. I've agreed to provide it; in fact, I'll get it out today. Is there anything else you need on this invoice?" There wasn't, so I changed the subject.

Interestingly, this exchange set the stage for one of the best client relationships I've ever had. When the owners realized that they weren't going to intimidate me (that I respected myself enough to prevent that from happening), they never challenged me again. We developed a rapport based on mutual respect that lasted for years. Self-respect opened the door to this long, mutually-rewarding relationship.

If it's difficult for you to stand your ground as I did, here's a book that can help you develop an attitude of self-respect. It's entitled *Winning Through Intimidation*.[8] Personally, I think the title should have been, Winning Through *Not* Being Intimidated. The author, Mr. Ringer, offers practical advice for dealing with people who would take advantage of you.

Self-respect means not allowing buyers to negotiate deals that are to your detriment. If you cave on a deal that you know is detrimental to you and your company, you've

- Demonstrated a lack of self-respect,
- Lost the buyer's respect,
- Invited the buyer to take further advantage of you.

---

[8] Robert Ringer, *Winning Through Intimidation*, Los Angeles Book Publishing, 1974

When you cave, the scales of justice tip in favor of the buyer. They continue to tip that way until you say, "No more!" This normally occurs when:

1. You try to negotiate a fair deal and the buyer refuses.
2. You walk away from the business because it's no longer profitable or only marginally profitable.
3. The buyer transfers her business to a competitor, someone she respects.

The outcome is the same for all three; *you lose the business*.

While your future and that of your company might be brighter without this business, in situations like this you should be asking yourself:

- Could I have avoided this situation by exercising greater self-respect?
- How much did it cost me and my company during the time we were doing business with this buyer?
- How did this situation influence my dealings with other buyers? Was I more aggressive? If so, did it cost me and my company business?
- Was my confidence shaken so much that I entered into more inequitable deals? If so, how much did they cost me and my company?
- Has this experience changed the market's perception of me and/or my company? If so, at what cost?

Respect yourself!
Not only will it help you build rapport with the buyer;
it will help you avoid hits to your bottom line.

There's one more element of rapport to consider, consistency. It doesn't matter how well we understand the first five; if we don't employ them consistently they have little value.

Consistency

The preceding five elements of rapport, genuine concern for others, understanding others' needs, respect, integrity and self-respect, must be demonstrated consistently. That doesn't mean that you have to be perfect. Buyers, at least the ones with whom you want to deal, forgive the occasional misstep, *if* you are otherwise consistent in your treatment of them.

How do you create consistency? Develop habits. If you're weak in one aspect of rapport building, choose an activity (just one) that will help you improve your skills in that area. Then engage in that activity every day for a month. By the end of the month, you'll have developed a habit; one that will serve you for years. Repeat the process every month with a new activity. You'll soon become a master rapport builder.

Consistency is the by-product of practice.

Let's review the key elements of rapport; they are:

1. Genuine concern for others
2. Understanding others' needs
3. Respect
4. Integrity
5. Self-respect
6. Consistency

You have complete control over their use. Let's see how you can use them to establish, strengthen or, heaven forbid, lose rapport with buyers.

Establishing Rapport

How will buyers know that you desire a long-term, mutually satisfying relationship? How will they know that you aren't just interested in making a sale? You begin answering these questions from the moment of your first contact.

Buyers know that you desire rapport when you:

- Give *without* expecting something in return
- Educate them (buyers)
- Focus on their needs/wishes, not the sale
- Help buyers overcome the obstacles they face
- Take care of buyers' emotional needs as well as their product/service needs

Let's explore each of these in more detail.

Give magnanimously

Be willing to share information that benefits the buyer. This goes beyond product/service information. You could provide an interesting perspective on the economy, information on a new technology or something more personal, like news about the buyer's favorite author or entertainer. This presumes that you're interested enough to discover her avocations.

Whatever you give, give without the expectation of receiving anything in return. If you expect the buyer to reciprocate, she will view your "gift" as self-serving. Conversely, if you give without expecting anything in return, she'll look for ways to repay your kindness.

We tend to reward those who are generous to us and withhold from those whose primary interest is their own welfare. Earn your reward. Give magnanimously!

For those of you who question whether anyone can truly give magnanimously, I'd like to share the wisdom of Jim Rohn, an internationally-renowned business and motivational speaker.

Mr. Rohn says that it's natural to expect something in return when we do a good deed; that's the way we're built. He also reminds us that "payment" usually doesn't come from the person for whom we do a good deed. Our reward usually comes sometime in the future from sources that we can't envision today.

I'm confident that you can recall instances where you have helped someone who couldn't help you. I'm also sure you can recall times when others helped you even though you couldn't return the favor. So what message can we take from these reflections? If you're patient enough to wait for a future reward, you can give magnanimously.

Mr. Rohn calls this type of giving enlightened self-interest. You're giving with the hope of getting a reward, but you realize that often the reward won't appear until sometime in the future, possibly from a source you wouldn't expect.

As buyers, you've encountered salespeople who expect an immediate return (the sale) and others who demonstrate a desire to see you make the right decision (magnanimous). What impression did you form about each of them? Did it affect your buying decision? The answers to these questions will guide your decision of whether to give magnanimously.

Educating the buyer is another form of giving. Let's see how it helps you establish rapport with your buyers.

Educate the buyer

Most buying decisions are *informed* decisions. What do I
mean by that? Most buyers won't make a buying decision
until they've gathered the information they need to feel
comfortable with their decision. The larger the price tag, the
more time the buyer spends gathering information.

Would you spend much time gathering information on a new
brand of canned corn? Why should you? The consequence
of a bad decision is small. The price of a can of corn is less
than a dollar. Besides losing the dollar, what's the worst that
can happen? You momentarily experience an unpleasant
flavor, throw away the corn and return to your old brand. No
big deal!

Buying canned corn is much different than buying your
company's first jet. A bad decision could cost your company
millions of dollars. That's why most people spend more time
researching the decision to buy a jet than they do buying a
can of corn. It also explains why grocery stores don't employ
salespeople while jet distributors do.

> *Educate your buyers. Help them make an informed*
> *decision. It's a great way to establish rapport.*

So far we've discussed giving magnanimously and educating
the buyer, now let's see where your focus should be, on the
buyer or the sale.

Focus on the buyer, not the sale

Your language will convey your motives. If you spend more
time talking about your product's/service's benefits than you
do the buyer's needs/interests, she'll know that you are more
interested in the sale than in her.

Conversely, when you communicate only those aspects of your offerings that interest her, she'll know that you are more interested in her than the sale. The psychological difference between these approaches is huge.

Let's say you're buying a new sound system and your primary interest is ease of installation. You've already determined that three brands offer satisfactory sound quality, now you're trying to determine which is easier to install.

Every time you ask the salesperson about installation, she offers some vague answer and returns to a discussion of sound quality. How do you feel? Do you like having your questions ignored? Do you like having someone impose *her* standards on *your* buying decision? How long will you tolerate this impudence? A salesperson using this approach usually loses the sale. Why? Her focus is wrong. She's obviously more interested in her product than the buyer.

When you communicate your offerings in light of your buyer's interests, you build rapport and increase the likelihood of making the sale.

Even when you successfully focus on the buyer's interests, the sale is a long way from being completed. Every buyer has obstacles to overcome. That's our next discussion.

Overcoming obstacles
Every buyer faces obstacles, things that prevent her from going ahead with the purchase. Some of these obstacles are:

- Budgetary constraints
- Lack of familiarity with the product/service
- Collegial/family influence

- More pressing issues
- An internal conflict between need and want

Acknowledge these obstacles, then help your buyer overcome them. How? Let's see.

Budgetary constraints
Have you ever postponed a purchase because it "wasn't in the budget?" Most of us have. What we don't realize is that these constraints are self-imposed, often subconsciously, but self-imposed.

Why do I say subconsciously? As buyers, we typically look at available cash, decide that we don't have enough and postpone the purchase. This decision involves subconscious acceptance of our current spending habits as inviolable. That's simply not true. The reality is that most of us simply don't take the time to evaluate our spending habits to see how we can afford something we want.

Successful salespeople know this. Here are some ways they help their buyers *without reducing the price of their offering.* They

- Help consumers explore their spending habits;
- Help business leaders reexamine budgets;
- Offer installment payments;
- Stage deliveries;
- Offer lower-priced alternatives.

Exploring spending habits and reexamining budgets are the same exercise. We just use different lingo depending upon whether we're serving consumers or businesses.

Installment payments allow us to enjoy something today while paying for it in the future. Staged deliveries allow buyers to commit to large future purchases while paying for small quantities, as delivered. Low-price alternatives are offerings which are in some way inferior to products/services you typically offer. These are only a few examples. My goal in listing them is to jumpstart your thinking about how you can deal with buyers' budgetary constraints.

> ***Want to endear yourself to buyers? Help them overcome their perceived budgetary constraints.***

Some of you may be surprised that I didn't list "lowering the price" as an option. In some instances, lowering your price can diminish the buyer's satisfaction with her purchase. If you're skeptical, check out Chapter 5, *Pricing*, where we explore misconceptions about pricing.

For now, let's turn our attention to the second obstacle buyers face, lack of familiarity with the product/service.

Lack of familiarity
You may be inclined to skip this section thinking that we've covered this information in the *Educate the buyer* section. I hope you'll resist that temptation because what we're going to discuss is the amount of information each buyer needs to make a decision. It varies dramatically from buyer to buyer.

If you're paying attention, your first few minutes with a buyer will tell you much information she needs to make a decision. If she asks tough questions, absorbs information quickly and responds quickly to your answers, she's all business. She wants only pertinent information and she wants it quickly; no small talk.

If she comments on family pictures or awards hanging on your wall, she wants to get to know you before she hears about your offerings. The personal relationship is more important than the product/service you offer.

A buyer who frequently pauses to assimilate the information you've provided needs time to make a decision. Often you build rapport by offering to "give her time to think" and letting her know where you'll be should she have questions.

If the buyer frequently asks you to elaborate on your answers or repeatedly asks the same questions, she's cautious. She'll probably have a difficult time making a decision. Repeating your answers over and over again can be frustrating for you, but it's absolutely essential to her if she is to feel comfortable with her purchase.

Don't try to be all things to all people. If you don't have the patience to handle the last situation, know which salespeople in your organization do and politely transfer the buyer to one of them. That way your company still has a shot at the sale.

Present information the way your buyer prefers. If you can't, refer her to a salesperson who can.

With budgetary constraints and lack of familiarity under our belts, let's turn our attention to the third obstacle buyers face, influence from their colleagues.

Collegial influence
This one's tough. Buyers don't often admit to external influence because it makes them appear weak. It's even tougher if the influencer isn't there. Her absence prevents you from helping the influencer confront her concerns.

When you sense this obstacle ask questions about how the buyer's decision will affect loved ones, her staff, her team or other areas of the company. The buyer often finds it easier to express her concerns about her decision's impact on others, than to admit that others are influencing her decision.

Every day your buyer interacts with family members, friends, colleagues and bosses, all of whom influence her decisions. Don't underestimate their influence.

Another reason why a buyer might not be taking action is that she's facing more pressing issues.

More pressing issues
Timing is essential in selling. More often than not, when the buyer says "No," she's rejecting the *timing* of your offer, not the offer itself. How can you tell when timing is the issue?

Ask yourself the following questions:

- Does the buyer's body language indicate interest?
- Has she asked for more information?
- Has she made statements indicating how she'll use your offering?

If you answered "Yes" to any of these questions, but the buyer still won't commit, explore the possibility that she's facing more pressing issues. How?

Ask her questions like, "How quickly would you like to see …(these benefits)?" or "You seem interested, but I sense some hesitation, are there other priorities that you're facing? If so, what are they?"

You could also ask her what time commitment she feels she'd be making if she bought your offering. Buyers are as likely to overestimate the time they'll invest as they are the budgetary constraints they face.

This approach opens the door for the buyer to reevaluate her priorities and, possibly, move your offering to the top of her list. Do that and you've not only set the stage for this sale, but for future sales as well.

> *It will be difficult to establish rapport with the buyer if you ignore the fact that she's facing a whole host of issues, some more pressing than the one your offering addresses.*

The last obstacle we're going to discuss deals with the age-old battle between what the buyer wants and what she needs.

Internal conflict
It's tough being an adult. We're constantly being asked to do the responsible thing, when what we really want to do is have fun. This conflict spills over into our buying decisions. We continually weigh decisions of whether to buy what we need or what we want. Your buyers face the same dilemma.

Help your buyer resolve this conflict. Help her clarify the issues in her own mind. You'll not only understand what's really important to her; you'll be able to help her make an informed decision. Sprinkle in some of the approaches you'd use in dealing with budgetary constraints and you're likely to find a way for the buyer to enjoy some of what she wants as well as what she needs. *Ch-Ching!* Another sale!

Help your buyer see that she can meet both her needs and wants and she's likely to reward you with the sale.

Armed with the knowledge of the obstacles buyers face and techniques for dealing with them, let's explore the final step in establishing rapport, buyers' emotional needs.

Emotional needs

In previous sections, we explored buyers' emotional needs. Everything from how much information they need to the highly-charged conflict between wants and needs; from the need to be respected to the desire to deal with someone they respect; from the desire to be educated to the wish that they not be "sold." These emotions are real and powerful. That's why effective sales managers keep driving home the point that *"buying decisions are made emotionally, not logically."* Your ability to establish rapport depends heavily on your ability to satisfy buyers' emotional needs.

Buying decisions are emotional decisions.

Even though you've established rapport, the job is far from over. You've got to nurture that rapport *if* you want to keep your competitors at bay.

Strengthening Rapport

Frequent contact with the buyer and consistent application of the *key elements of rapport* are what's needed to strengthen rapport. I'll repeat the key elements here so that you don't waste time trying to refresh your memory. The key elements of rapport are:

1. Genuine concern for others
2. Understanding others' needs

3. Respect
4. Integrity
5. Self-respect
6. Consistency

I'm sure you understand the need for consistent application of these elements, but you're probably wondering how often you should be contacting the buyer. Again, we look to the individual's emotional needs for guidance:

- Buyers who are all business may only want to be contacted once or twice a year *unless* you have something new that will help them.
- Buyers who value personal relationships in their business dealings may want to be contacted every month or two.
- Buyers who require time to decide are often shy and retiring; limit your contacts to three or four times a year. When you do make contact, make it a friendly visit or an educational meeting. *Don't try to sell.* You can lose rapport with them very quickly by trying to make another sale.
- Buyers who require incredible amounts of detail before deciding are most happy when involved in projects that they can do alone. Ask them how often they'd like to be contacted; it usually won't be more than once or twice a year. It's difficult to develop much less sustain rapport with these buyers; don't be too hard on yourself if you're finding it difficult to strengthen your relationship with this type of buyer.

Allow your buyers and prospects to participate in the decision concerning your next contact with them; they'll find it difficult to fault you for being overly zealous.

I hope that it's obvious that most of the rapport strengthening contacts should demonstrate your interest and concern for the individual. This concern can be expressed in many different forms, providing information specific to the buyer's business, making her aware of upcoming events that would interest her, asking how she enjoyed her vacation.

These contacts should not be disguised sales calls. Buyers know that one of the reasons you're contacting them is to generate more sales; they're not naïve. Yet, they resent the contact only when they sense your primary interest is the sale, not them. Disguising a sales call as a friendly contact is one sure way to lose rapport. Let's look at some others.

Losing Rapport

It's easy! Place your interests ahead of the buyer's. Respond slowly to their phone calls and requests. Allow the buyer's problems to go unresolved. Stop sending periodic thank-you notes. Lie to your buyers. Ask them to make decisions based solely on their trust in you. Fail to contact them as frequently as they desire. This is the short list!

The sad reality is that salespeople often do these horrible things *without* malicious intent. Why? They, like the rest of us, take for granted the good relationships we have with others. We forget that they need nurturing. That's not malicious, but it is foolish. It's a pitfall you need to avoid.

What's interesting is that successful salespeople seldom stumble on rapport establishing steps. Their missteps almost always occur with existing customers, the buyers with whom they are most familiar. Don't allow this to happen to you.

Make sure that the first entries in next year's calendar are contact dates with existing customers. Schedule contact frequency based on each customer's stated preference.

We have a sense for the importance of rapport, but what benefits do we actually gain for all this effort?

The Benefits of Rapport

Rapport generates benefits well beyond the profits of the pending sale. First, there's the obvious value of the buyer's business over the life of the relationship.

Second, buyers with whom you have rapport often tell you what sales approaches your competitors are using. They'll also alert you to any advantage your competitors are gaining, whether it's through technology, pricing or service offerings. This knowledge helps you employ preemptive strikes that can protect buyer relationships where your rapport isn't as strong as you'd like it to be.

Third, you'll learn that buyers have found new uses for your offerings. I can't tell you how often I see products/services being used for purposes other than their original design. If you aren't taking an interest in your buyer's business, if you are not walking around her plant, you won't discover new uses for your offerings. It's one of the most valuable and often-overlooked benefits rapport offers.

If you're interested in learning more about your competitors' strategies and alternative uses for your offerings, build rapport with your customers. They'll share this information with you.

Other Misconceptions

Salespeople tend to look at good buyer relationships as fixed, unchanging landscapes. In reality, change is imminent.

Employee Turnover

Ask your buyers to introduce you to their colleagues in other departments, then develop rapport with these folks as well. Why? Employee turnover is incredibly high these days, as evidenced by the frequent downsizings and rightsizings in large and small corporations alike. Unless you have good rapport with multiple contacts in an organization, it's going to be difficult to retain that organization's business.

Family Relationships

If you sell *personal* products/services, it's important to understand how the family's age composition affects buying decisions. Children gain more influence as they mature, often becoming the decision-makers for their parents in later years. Unless you develop rapport with the buyer's family members, you'll very likely lose business as decision-making responsibilities shift.

Before we move onto Chapter 4, *Customer Service*, I want to explain why I have chosen not to discuss selling techniques in this book. There are many excellent programs and books that teach you how to prospect, how to use questions, how to create urgency and how to close. If you're interested in these techniques, I'd recommend that you read *How to Master the Art of Selling*,[9] *Visionary Selling*[10] and *The Sales Bible*.[11]

---

[9] Tom Hopkins, *How to Master the Art of Selling*, Warner Books, 1982
[10] Barabara Geraghty, *Visionary Selling*, Simon & Schuster, 1998
[11] Jeffrey Gitomer, *The Sales Bible*, William Morrow, HarperCollins

Core Concept – Selling

The key to every
successful sales effort
is to build rapport with
the buyer so that your
competitors find it
difficult to get in the door.

Executive Summary – Selling

- There are six keys to building rapport:

  1. Genuine concern for others
  2. Understanding others' needs
  3. Respect
  4. Integrity
  5. Self-respect
  6. Consistency

- To establish rapport:

  1. Give *without* expecting something in return
  2. Educate buyers
  3. Focus on buyers' wishes, not the sale
  4. Help buyers overcome obstacles they face
  5. Take care of buyers' emotional needs as well as their product/service needs

- Obstacles buyers face are:

  1. Budgetary constraints
  2. Lack of familiarity with the product/service
  3. Collegial influence
  4. More pressing issues
  5. Conflict between needs and wants

- The benefits of rapport are measured by:

  1. The value of the buyer's business over the life of the relationship
  2. Information about competitors' strategies
  3. News about alternative uses for your offerings

Now that your salespeople have rapport with their buyers, let's make sure the rest of the organization doesn't squirrel the relationship for them.

"You said it would be here by 9:00 a.m."

That's customer service's role! Or is it? We'll answer that question in Chapter 4, *Customer Service*.

CUSTOMER SERVICE:

A wild ride!

4

Customer Service

What is the goal of every successful customer service effort?

**To strengthen the customer rapport developed
by your salespeople.**

Core Concept – Enhance Rapport

Remember when you were a kid and your parents took you to
the fair? Remember the roller coaster? Depending on your
constitution, you're either sporting a broad smile or holding
your stomach. Your experience was either exhilarating or
nauseating; there's nothing in between.

As a business leader, customer service is your roller coaster ride. Only this time a strong constitution won't save you from nausea. There will be times when, despite your best efforts, your employees will irritate your customers. It's a fact of life! It's going to happen! The most you can do is minimize the nausea.

Why should customer service be so difficult? Why should it be so hard to assure the customer's happiness when you and your employees *know* what *you* expect in the way of service? The answers to these questions fall into three categories:

- Conflicting goals
- Communication missteps
- Work environment

Before we explore each of these categories, let's discuss the evolution of customer service.

Evolution Of Customer Service

Historically, customer service representatives have dealt with customer complaints. The problem with this approach is that you're relying on the customer to complain. Many don't; they simply take their business elsewhere.

Today, customer service reps take an active role; they initiate customer contacts. They call the customer shortly after the sale to make sure that he's pleased with his purchase or the service he's received. He's asked to comment on how he was treated by each of the company's representatives. While this approach helps you identify problems more quickly, it still has disadvantages.

1. It's retrospective; you're still examining the customer experience after the purchase.
2. This system is usually linked to a reward/punishment system with greater emphasis on punishment than reward. If, as an employee, you drop the ball too often, you're out of a job. If you satisfy the customer 98% of the time, you're simply doing your job.
3. Many customers abhor confrontation. They don't voice their displeasure; they vote with their feet.

As you can see, traditional customer service approaches have severe limitations. What's the solution? Abandon the myth that customer service is a departmental responsibility. Make your customer's welfare *every* employee's job. The entire organization needs to have the customer as its primary focus. That's where we begin our discussion.

Organizational Focus

Customer service is an attitude, an attitude that should be demonstrated by *each and every one of your employees, everyday*. It should be obvious to your customers that all of your employees embrace the six elements of rapport:

1. Genuine concern for others
2. Understanding others' needs
3. Respect
4. Integrity
5. Self-respect
6. Consistency

No, I'm not talking just about salespeople and customer service reps. I'm talking about the credit and collection folks, production staff, warehouse crew and accounting

group. Are they incorporating rapport-building into their
decision-making process? Probably not. Why?

The answer lies in their focus. They don't see themselves
serving the customer; they're speeding collections, improving
quality, getting the goods out the door or reporting results. In
their minds, the sales force and customer service people are
responsible for customer relationships.

Are they right? Not when you consider the impact their
decisions have on the customer's experience. How does it
affect the customer's experience when the:

- Credit people make the application process tedious
- Quality people over-promise and under-deliver
- Warehouse workers ship the wrong item or ship late
- Accounting people establish more stringent payment
  terms to improve cash flow

You can see that every employee has the potential to impact a
customer's experience. Yet, few employees are aware of the
impact they're having. Why is that? Here's a hint. Look at
the goals they're being asked to achieve.

Conflicting Goals

As a business leader you strive to achieve two goals that
inherently conflict with one another. You recognize the need
to "Wow!" customers, but you also need to control costs *if*
your company is to be profitable. What does this do to an
organization? It often results in a battle, sales and customer
service reps vs. your operations people.

"It's the customer vs. cost control!"

Your salespeople and customer service reps want customers to be absolutely delighted with your offerings; so much so, that the customer wouldn't think of going anywhere else. At the same time your operating managers are looking for ways to reduce costs, often without regard for the customer. Here are a few examples of the conflicts that occur.

Salespeople, who rely on rapid response to differentiate your company's offerings, wonder why the shipping department keeps dropping the ball. The folks in shipping wonder why the sales force continues to sell rapid response when shipping is being pressured to reduce costs.

Credit and collection people are expected to be cautious in granting credit and aggressive in collecting receivables. In fact, their bonuses are often determined by the age of the receivables and amount of bad debt write-offs. How do these goals jibe with your desire to delight the customer?

Accounting people, under pressure to reduce transaction costs, move to a paperless billing system *without* seeking customer input. Can you imagine the headaches they'll cause for your customers?

I could go on, but you get the picture. How do you deal with this conflict between customer service and cost reduction? Here are a few tips.

Conflict prevention
Avoid the conflict! Decide which is more valuable to you, customer loyalty or cost reduction? While these are not mutually exclusive goals, there are trade-offs.

Generally, loyal customers generate more profits than cost reduction efforts. Why? Loyal customers typically aren't price buyers which means they don't object to higher prices. Higher prices result in better margins and a stronger bottom line. Loyal customers are also likely to refer their family, friends and colleagues, opening the door for more business.

Conversely, cost reductions usually are temporary. Talk to the leaders of even the most successful companies and they'll tell you it's extremely difficult to sustain cost savings.

When customer service becomes your number one priority, communicate that decision to your entire workforce. That's right, everyone in the company. The examples above show quite vividly how your employees' decisions can influence customer rapport. Communicate your decision to everyone. We'll discuss some of the more common communication missteps later; for now, let's make sure that everyone in the company knows that customer service is your top priority.

Demonstrate your commitment to balancing customer service and cost reduction. How? Whenever you're presented with a cost reduction strategy, ask, "How's this going to impact our customers?" You'll only have to ask the question a few times before your direct reports get the idea that customer rapport must be considered in every cost reduction initiative.

Finally, include your customers in your cost reduction efforts. Does that make you feel a little uncomfortable? Are you afraid that your customers are going to want price reductions when they learn that you're saving money? It's possible, but there are ways to avoid this problem which we'll discuss in a few minutes.

Make sure that everyone in the organization considers your customers' needs BEFORE making a decision.

In this section we've been discussing what we need to do to align the goals of all departments with the customers' needs. By focusing all decisions on customers' needs, we avoid the conflict between customer service and cost reduction, but that isn't the only conflict we face.

Interdepartmental conflict

As they get larger, organizations become departmentalized according to specialty, marketing, R & D, accounting, human resources. The focus of each department narrows to reflect this specialization. The unfortunate and often-overlooked effect is that the customer's needs get lost.

If that isn't bad enough, departmentalization often results in interdepartmental conflict. How? Each department creates its goals without regard to the impact those goals will have on other departments. This is called the silo effect. Silos are built gradually. As organizations grow, as the focus of each department narrows, the silos get taller and taller.

The silo effect explains why

- Conflicting goals exist within organizations;
- Department heads view the world as a zero-sum game, someone must lose for them to win;
- Business leaders often find themselves drawn into interdepartmental conflicts;
- Employee productivity suffers.

These nasty effects can be avoided *if* focusing all employees' attention on the customers' needs. Make the customer the primary focus of your employees' decision-making process. Help your employees understand the impact their decisions will have on other departments' ability to serve the customer. In the process, you'll avoid many of the interdepartmental conflicts other companies experience.

When employees are focused on the customer, their goals align naturally, avoiding much of the internal conflict found in most companies.

Earlier I promised to provide some tips that would allow you to involve your customers in cost reduction strategies without inviting a request for lower prices. Here they are.

Involve your customers
Cost reduction doesn't help your customers *unless* you lower your price. So why would you want your customers to help you reduce costs? You don't! You want them to help you improve your product's quality or the service you provide them. Cost reduction is a natural byproduct of quality/service improvements, especially when you involve the customer. I'd be surprised if you weren't at least a little skeptical. Let's take a look at what happens when you involve your customer.

You approach your customers with the request that they help you serve them better. You ask that they work with you to identify quality and service needs they have that they haven't expressed. Then collaboratively you explore ways to honor their requests. In the process you'll learn:

- What aspects of your offering have little, if any, value to them; these can be eliminated, often with price concessions much smaller than your cost savings (I didn't say you should never give a price concession).
- What your customer really wants; is there anything more expensive than developing an offering that isn't wanted by the market?
- About inefficiencies in your systems; their removal will save you money.
- How your customers have successfully dealt with inefficiencies in their organizations that exist in yours; another way to save money.
- What inefficiencies exist in your customers' systems that you've successfully addressed in your company; this will save them money and reduce the likelihood they'll seek price concessions from you.

That's why I say that cost reductions are a natural byproduct of quality and service improvements, but that's not the whole story. In addition you'll learn:

- How your customers needs are evolving so that you can position yourself to meet those needs *before* your competitors do.
- How your customers' customers' needs are evolving; giving you greater lead time for developing offerings.
- Alternative uses for your offerings, a wonderful way to increase the number of markets served.

How's that for a return on your investment? Besides these substantial returns your customers get the sense that you:

- Genuinely care about them
- Value their judgement
- Are continuously trying to improve your operations

Your customers also:

- Have advance notice of changes in your offerings and how those changes will impact them
- Have input into the form those changes will take
- Understand the reasons behind the changes
- Are more receptive to those changes

All of this presumes that you and your customer have a mutually respectful working relationship. This approach won't work with customers who are continually trying to take advantage of you. That's okay; you shouldn't be dealing with someone like that anyway.

Involve your customers in quality and service improvement efforts, not cost reduction strategies.

We've discussed the conflict between customer needs and cost reduction, interdepartmental conflicts and the value of involving your customers in quality/service improvements. It's time to discuss the impact compensation programs have on customer satisfaction.

Compensation
Align your compensation programs with your customer service focus. Nothing that you say will carry the weight your compensation program does. How can I be so sure?

During a training program the client's employees related a problem they were experiencing. As I began to explore their predicament they said, "Oh, we know how to fix it!" I'm sure my astonishment was evident as I asked, "Why do you allow the problem to continue?" They said, "That's not how we're bonused."

Money isn't the only motivator, but it certainly influences your employees' decisions. Given a choice between their families' welfare and the company's welfare, employees usually choose their families.

Base your employees' compensation on goals designed to enhance your customers' experience.

Let's do a quick review. You can avoid the conflict between customer service and cost reduction by:

1. Choosing to make your customers' needs everyone's top priority
2. Aligning your employees' goals with your customers' needs
3. Involving your customers in quality/service improvement strategies
4. Assuring that customer service is given a lot of weight when designing compensation plans

You can do all of these things well and still lose the customer service battle. How? Through poor communication!

Communication Missteps
How many of these missteps have you experienced?

1. Phone calls or e-mails not being returned
2. Endless waiting on the phone
3. Website answers for everything but your question
4. Customer service people who lack the authority to solve your problem
5. Customer service reps who fake it when they don't know the answer
6. Three or more phone transfers attempting to get you to the *right* department
7. Voice mail that doesn't allow personal contact
8. Customer service people who believe you're wrong until proven right
9. Unfulfilled promises
10. Customer service reps who express a "take it or leave it" attitude
11. Customer service people who make you do the bulk of the work in resolving the problem
12. Customer service reps who string you along instead of delivering an unpleasant message
13. Customer service people who fail to give you all the information you need, causing you to make yet another call

Did this baker's dozen stir some unpleasant memories? If so, you have a sense of the frustration your customers experience when your employees make one of these communication missteps. How do you avoid them? Let's see what some of the premier customer service companies do.

Learning from the best
Take cues from the best in customer service, Nordstrom, Ritz-Carlton and PSS/World Medical. They've done an excellent job of avoiding most communication missteps. I say "most" because no one's perfect. Occasionally their

employees choose the wrong words or miss an opportunity to enhance a customer's experience. Before we see how the leaders in these companies keep communication missteps to a minimum, let's examine the foundation of their customer service philosophies.

Even though Nordstrom, Ritz-Carlton and PSS/World Medical represent three very different industries (retail, hospitality, medical), they have very similar approaches to customer service. Here are the keys to their success:

1. Every employee is devoted to making the customer happy or they don't remain employed at these companies.
2. Employees receive extensive training to help them develop a customer service mentality.
3. Customer's needs must be satisfied *immediately.*
4. Employees have the authority to spend money to satisfy customer needs.
5. Employees are recognized and rewarded for exceptional customer service.

Each of these customer service imperatives requires clear, consistent communication daily. These communications go beyond the spoken word. Employees of Nordstrom, Ritz-Carlton and PSS Medical communicate their dedication to service by their attitudes and behavior. Every employee in these organizations is expected to model the behavior everyday. That's how Nordstrom, Ritz-Carlton and PSS Medical distinguish themselves with their customer service.

If you want your employees to make customer service their top priority, you have to tell them every day in a variety of ways. How? Again, we can learn from the best. Here are some of the tools they use:

- Personal mission statements; employees create mission statements for themselves that support the company's mission
- Daily affirmation; every day employees affirm their commitment to customer service
- Spot recognition/reward programs; employees are recognized or rewarded on the spot for exceptional customer service
- Company-wide recognition programs; employees receive company-wide acclaim for their efforts
- Training; employees receive extensive training reinforced by the techniques just described - daily affirmations, spot recognition/reward programs and company-wide recognition programs
- Promotions based on customer service
- Compensation based on customer service

What happens when you apply these tools daily? Your employees find it difficult to forget what's important to the customer. Their minds become so focused on the customer that they rarely make the communication missteps listed above. That's how you avoid these missteps; that's how you enhance the rapport your sales force developed.

Communication missteps typically occur when your employees aren't focused on the customer.

Some of you may be feeling a little uncomfortable right now. You're wondering, "How can the leaders at Nordstrom, Ritz-Carlton and PSS trust so many people to make the right decision?" I can tell you they don't trust blindly. Here's how they develop that trust.

Learning to trust

First, prospective employees go through rigorous screening to assure that new hires share the values their companies do.

Second, they train extensively. All three companies invest heavily in customer service training, which dramatically reduces their risk.

Third, leaders and peers provide *daily* feedback to employees so that they know how well they're performing and what they can do to improve. This practice accelerates the employee's learning and reinforces the customer service message.

Fourth, the leaders of these companies *expect* employees to act responsibly. Patrick Kelly of PSS/World Medical says that each of his employees has CEO on their business card because when they are in front of the customer they are the company. If you were an employee at PSS, how would a statement like that influence your actions? Would you want to disappoint someone who views you as a CEO? Of course not! You'll work hard to live up to their expectations.

These four practices, rigorous screening, extensive training, daily feedback and high expectations, make it easier for the employee to make the right decision which allows their leaders to trust their decisions.

***It's easy to trust your employees
when you know their values and train them well.***

Hopefully you've noticed that the quality of communication between employees and customers depends heavily on the quality of communications between employees and leaders. It's the constant communication of values, expectations and results by leaders that allows employees to communicate effectively with your customers and serve them well.

The quality of communication between employee and customer depends heavily on the quality of communication between employee and leader.

It's difficult for employees to maintain an attitude of service when their work environment isn't supporting them. Let's see just how important the work environment is.

Work Environment

When do you feel most generous - when you've just received a windfall or when you're struggling to pay your bills? Your answer offers insights into how employees' attitudes toward customers are shaped by their work environment.

Let's say that you just had a discussion with your boss and found that he genuinely cares about you, respects you and values your judgement. How do you feel? What's your attitude toward the rest of humanity? Are you more forgiving of other people's quirks? Does it take a little longer for an unintended slight to irritate you? Why is that?

You're experiencing a windfall, an emotional windfall. The world is a wonderful place because you've had a wonderful experience. It's natural to want to share that feeling with others and you will. You'll be generous with your praise, encouraging with your colleagues and supportive of someone who's struggling.

Would your attitude be the same if your boss just blasted you for missing an unrealistic deadline and a co-worker failed to get you information you need for *another* pressing deadline? What's your demeanor likely to be, something akin to a bear awakening from hibernation? Of course! Your emotional reserves are depleted! How easy is it going to be for you to show care and concern for others? Not likely, is it? You simply don't have the emotional energy to draw upon.

These simple examples illustrate how important it is for your work environment to *continuously* provide emotional energy to your employees. It's not something you want to leave to chance, especially if you want your employees to dedicate themselves to exceptional customer service.

> *Your company's work environment has the capacity to infuse or drain emotional energy from your employees.*

How do you create a work environment that infuses energy?" Chapter 8, *Work Environment*, answers that question.

Even though you and your employees know what good customer service is, it will be difficult to achieve unless you:

1. Choose customer service over cost control
2. Minimize the silo effect
3. Minimize communication missteps by improving your communications with employees
4. Create a work environment that infuses energy to your workforce

If you think "that's just too much work," you've bought into another misconception about customer service. The payback isn't worth the investment.

Other Misconceptions

If you're not sure whether investing in great customer service is worth the effort, take a look at these benefits.

Benefits

Obviously, there's a lot of work involved in providing exceptional customer service, but the paybacks are huge. Some of the ways your customers reward you are:

- Repeat business
- Referrals
- Premium prices

These rewards are significant. Since they're also fairly obvious, I'll keep the discussion to a minimum.

Repeat business

How would you like to reduce your selling costs while increasing sales? That's what happens when you get lots of repeat orders from existing customers. You save on selling costs because:

- Rapport already exists; your sales force can use the time they would have spent building rapport to accept orders and further enhance the customer relationship.
- Fewer mistakes are made on repeat orders than new orders. That's true whether you're examining error rates in production, shipping or billing.

These are two powerful reasons for investing in customer service, but they're only the tip of the iceberg.

Referrals
Another way to keep selling costs down is to call on people who want your offerings. Millions of sales calls each year are wasted on prospects who don't need the product or service they're being offered. That's expensive!

Referrals bring qualified buyers to your salespeople; they don't have to spend so much time searching for them. Plus it takes less time for your salesperson to establish rapport with the buyer. He has immediate credibility thanks to the referral source. All of these factors combine to shorten the selling cycle which keeps selling costs down.

The third benefit comes from pricing, not cost savings.

Premium prices
In Chapter 3, *Selling*, we discussed the fact that over 80% of the buying public does not consider price one of the top five criteria in their buying decision. Things like quality, timely delivery, convenience, courtesy, respect and friendliness are more important to the vast majority of buyers.

As we look at this list, it's obvious that the majority of these items fit into the broader category of customer service. What that tells us is that great customer service is more important than price. In effect, customers are telling us that it's okay to charge a higher price *if* we meet their other needs. Higher prices mean higher profits.

Repeat business, referrals and premium prices offer some very compelling reasons to make the investment in great customer service, if you haven't already. Even if you have, it may be worthwhile to explore ways to enhance your already successful efforts.

Earlier in this chapter we explored the conflicting goals companies face, customer service vs. cost control. Not all of these conflicts are internally-generated.

Externally-Generated Conflict

Sometimes you don't get to choose the balance you want between customer service and cost control. PSS/World Medical, Inc. found itself facing this dilemma.[12]

PSS World Medical was the premier provider of medical supplies to physicians' offices in the United States. The keys to their success were same day delivery and strong personal relationships. PSS was rewarded for their efforts with a premium price. In Mr. Kelly's words, PSS was the Mercedes of the industry.

In 1993, shortly after former President Bill Clinton and his wife, Hillary, launched their health-care initiative, PSS customer surveys showed that their customers were more interested in low prices than premium service. The problem was that their customers had already become accustomed to extraordinary service. Anything less would have been disappointing *even though the price was lower*.

PSS was suddenly faced with the challenge of maintaining existing service levels on lower margins. You can imagine the budget battles that must have ensued, the sales forces' dismay at the possibility of earning less and the shift in

---

[12] Patrick Kelly, *Faster Company*, Wiley & Sons, 1998

organizational mindset that had to occur to provide both exceptional service and low prices. Yet, the folks at PSS successfully negotiated all these hurdles. How? By focusing on their customers!

They never lost sight of the fact that great customer service pays in more ways than premium prices. They found ways to reduce costs without impacting the customer. Yes, PSS suffered some short-term profit declines and their leaders and employees weathered salary reductions, but they found ways to keep their customers happy. Their efforts kept the door open for PSS to find more ways to serve these customers, to find ways to replace the revenues lost through lower prices.

I doubt that PSS could have managed the transition from premium pricing to cost reduction if they had not had a history of exceptional customer service.

Whether internally or externally generated, conflicts between customer service and cost control are easier to deal with when you already have a strong customer focus.

Before we move onto Chapter 5, *Pricing*, let's review the core concept of customer service.

Core Concept – Customer Service

> **The goal of every successful customer service effort is to strengthen the rapport developed by your salespeople.**

We've dealt with a couple of pricing myths thus far. Let's see if there are any more. Join me in Chapter 5, *Pricing.*

Executive Summary – Customer Service

- Most customer service problems can be traced to:

  1. Conflicting goals
  2. Communication missteps
  3. Work environment

- Conflicting goals - As business leaders you face two goals that are inherently in conflict with one another, customer service and cost control.

- Communication missteps – Your employees are less likely to make communication missteps with your customers if their attention is focused on customer service *every day*.

- Work environment – Your company's work environment can either infuse or drain emotional energy from your employees. If you infuse energy, the customer will be treated well; if you drain energy, the customer will suffer.

- There are tremendous benefits to be gained from providing great customer service. Here's what you can expect:

  1) Repeat business from existing customers
  2) New customers from referrals
  3) Premium prices

  With the first two, you have the opportunity to increase sales while reducing your selling costs. The third offers an opportunity to increase your profit margins.

PRICING :

Are you leaving money on the table?

5

Pricing

What is the goal of every successful pricing policy?

To be compensated well for the value you provide, while giving greater value than you receive.

Core Concept – Value

Would you like to find a quick, inexpensive way to increase profits? Raise your prices! What's that? Easier said than done? That's how a lot of business leaders feel. It's also one of the great myths in business.

During the past 13 years, I've seen far too many clients who are woefully under-compensated for the value they provide.

Why? Here are some of the explanations they offer.

- My competitors won't let me.
- I don't have the name awareness the big boys do.
- Competitor's customers won't talk to me unless I offer them lower prices.
- My goal is greater market share.
- The market is shrinking.

We'll address each of these "explanations" later, *after* we gain a better understanding of the connection between price and value. Why start there? The price/value comparison is the focus of every buying decision.

The Buying Decision

You make buying decisions every day. In each and every one of these decisions, you weigh the value you'll get vs. the price you're asked to pay. You buy when the value is greater than the price; you pass when it isn't. It's that simple.

Most buying decisions are made subconsciously. You're not aware that you're making the price/value comparison. Why? Most of your purchases are repetitive, involving small-ticket items. Yet, the price/value comparison is made in every one of these decisions. Still not convinced?

Let's say that you're visiting your favorite ice cream stand. You order your usual, a whopping $2.50 purchase. The counter person says, "That'll be $2.75." How do you react? Do you hesitate?

"That'll be $2.75"

Of course you do. It may only be for a second, but you'll hesitate before paying a meager 25¢ price increase. Why? You're making the price/value comparison. You want to make sure the enjoyment you'll get is worth the additional price. It's a natural reaction! It's the way we're built.

The price/value comparison is made in EVERY purchase.

Our example demonstrates that buyers are making these comparisons, but it doesn't help us understand what they value. We need additional information to determine that.

What Customers Value
In order to determine what price customers will pay, we need to know what they value. This can be a daunting task. Why?

There are so many things buyers value including low prices, dependability, quality, quick delivery, convenience, courtesy, friendliness, selection, ambience, and that's the short list!

In an attempt to serve their customers, sellers create offerings that provide several of the benefits listed above. The more benefits an offering provides, the more difficult it becomes to discern what customers truly value. That's why pricing feels like guesswork to so many sellers.

How can we help these sellers? More importantly, how can you discover what your customers really value? Treacy and Wiersema's, *The Discipline of Market Leaders*,[13] provides an approach that'll help you answer that question.

As discussed in Chapter 1, *Strategy*, Treacy and Wiersema found that the things buyers value fall nicely into three categories (value propositions):

- Low-cost
- Innovation
- Customer intimacy

Each value proposition represents a different market and, as you'll soon see, a different approach to pricing. Before we tackle pricing, let's make sure we understand the trade-offs a customer makes when choosing a value proposition. It'll help us understand the price/value comparison the customer is making.

Trade-offs
It's all about trade-offs. Customers who prefer low cost are usually willing to forego the latest innovation and some level of service to get the lower price.

---

[13] Michael Treacy & Fred Wiersema, *The Discipline of Market Leaders*, Addison-Wesley Publishing, 1995

Those who value innovation care less about price or customer service. They get their thrill from being on the leading edge of whatever new technology interests them.

Customers who value incredible service are typically willing to pay a higher price and forego the latest technology for the service experience they desire.

Treacy and Wiersema are quick to point out that each of us vacillates between these three value propositions depending upon what we're buying.

Once you understand these trade-offs, the question is which of these customers do you want to serve?

Which customer to serve

How do you decide which customer to serve? Treacy and Wiersema suggest that you look at your company's strength. If the people in your company excel at driving down costs, target the low cost market. If your employees love creating new offerings, target customers who value innovation. If your employees delight in creating memorable experiences, target the customer-intimate group.

Once you've identified the customers your company is best equipped to serve, you have the foundation of an effective pricing policy. Before we move onto the specifics of setting prices, let's get a sense for what each of these buyers expects in the way of pricing.

Pricing Overview

Here's a quick and dirty comparison of the pricing strategies for each of the three customer groups.

Buyer	Price expectation
Low-cost	A price that's lower than your competitors' prices (how's that for stating the obvious?)
Innovation	A price that's 4 to 6 times its market acceptance price (the price the offering commands when its accepted by a significant percentage of the market) and 10 times its market maturity price (the price the offering commands as it nears the end of its life)
Customer intimacy	A price that's some multiple of the price asked by competitors who don't provide the service you do

As you can see, pricing varies dramatically depending upon which customer group you serve. Now, it's time to be more specific about how to set prices for each group.

I'm sure that many of you are hoping that I'll provide a simple formula for you to use in establishing a price for your offerings. Unfortunately, there is no magic formula. There are too many factors that influence the buyer's decision, the economy, stock market performance and job security to name just a few. On top of that, there are the buyer's emotional needs to consider. All of these factors combine to make pricing more art than science.

While I can't provide you with formulas, I can provide you with thought processes you can employ in establishing prices for each of the three customer groups. Let's explore the elements involved in pricing for a low-cost buyer.

Low Cost

How do you set prices for a low cost buyer? Obviously your price needs to be lower than your competitors' prices, but how much lower? Keep in mind that you want to be compensated well even though you are providing low prices. To know how low to go, you need to answer two questions.

1. Who are your competitors?
2. What are you asking the buyer to forego?

Your competitors

On the surface, "Who are your competitors?" seems like an easy question. Your competitors are those companies that are offering products/services similar to the ones you're offering, right? Not if you talk to Herb Kelleher, the delightfully zany Chairman of Southwest Airlines. He says they're competing against the automobile. How's that for a paradigm shift?

The way Mr. Kelleher views competition offers a couple of valuable lessons. First, don't be afraid to change the rules. It may just be what's needed to leapfrog your competitors and *profitably* gain significant market share. Southwest is proof that it can be done.

Second, your competition in the future may not come from your current competitors. Do you think the major airlines expected Southwest to accomplish what it did?

Competition often comes from unexpected realms. Your company may find itself competing with companies that didn't previously exist or were never expected to evolve the way they did. Don't let your lead over existing competitors lull you into a false sense of security. There are many other companies out there looking for new markets to serve.

***Your competitors aren't always the companies offering
products/services similar to yours.***

How you view your competition can dramatically influence
the price you get for your offerings. You'll get a better feel
for that as we continue the Southwest example, but first, let's
explore the second question listed above, "What are you
asking the buyer to forego?"

Buyers' trade-offs

In order to offer a lower price, you typically have to ask the
customer to forego something. Why? Two reasons:

1. Every aspect of your offering has a cost. That cost
   has to be recovered either through cost control or
   higher prices.
2. Most companies aren't adept at cost control. If you
   doubt that, think about the number, magnitude and
   frequency of the downsizings reported by the Fortune
   500 in the last 15 years. These companies have the
   financial resources, talent and technology to *reduce*
   costs, yet they repeatedly fail to even *control* costs.

I hate repeating myself, but this point needs emphasis. Most
of the business leaders in corporate America do *not* get their
jollies from controlling costs. Don't trust me on this; list the
names of companies you know that are consistently profitable
using a low-price strategy.

How many were you able to name? Can you count them on
the fingers of one hand? One thing is certain, that number is
only a small percentage of the Fortune 500 companies. It's
folly to think that your company and your industry are any

different. The odds against your company excelling at cost control are very small.

A low-price strategy requires buyers to make a trade-off.

Let's continue our Southwest Airlines example to see what kinds of trade-offs buyers make and what impact these trade-offs have on pricing.

Southwest example

What trade-offs are Southwest's customers evaluating? It depends on whether they're planning to travel by plane or car. Here are some of the trade-offs for each mode of travel.

	Southwest vs. Other airlines	Southwest vs. Automobile
Convenience	Assigned seating vs. open seating	Airport vs. traffic
Time	Frequency of flights (Time at work vs. time at airport	Time traveling vs. time at destination
Work	Ability to work on plane (Southwest flies smaller planes making working conditions less comfortable than on other airlines)	Ability to work on plane vs. ability to work in car
Comfort	Physical comfort (Southwest flies smaller planes than other airlines)	Piloted travel vs. driver fatigue and passenger boredom
Atmosphere	Friendly vs. business	Limited visibility vs. sightseeing opportunities

	Southwest vs. Other airlines	Southwest vs. Automobile
Amenities	Peanuts vs. in-flight meals	In-flight restroom facilities vs. harried search for facilities
Cost	Southwest's low fares vs. other airlines fares	Southwest's fare plus ground transportation vs. cost of driving and lodging during transit

How do these trade-offs influence pricing? Let's compare several situations.

Buyer preferences	Price concession desired on a $500 roundtrip ticket
Business flyer wants to be in and out in the same day, doesn't mind waiting in line to board and hates airline food	$30 to $50
Business flyer wants to use every available second in airport and on plane to work, is tall, will have an overnight stay regardless of flight frequency, considers the food a distraction from work	$100 to $125
Recreational traveler planning a trip to see new grandbaby, enjoys air travel so much that other aspects of flying like boarding and meals are unimportant	$15 to $25

Buyer preferences	Price concession desired on a $500 roundtrip ticket
Recreational traveler plans vacation that takes her through some of America's most scenic areas (places she's always wanted to see), sightseeing during travel and at destination are equally important	Price is not a consideration in this decision
Recreational traveler enjoys driving, but is weighing the advantages of spending more time at her destination vs. the driving enjoyment; wants an enjoyable experience whichever mode of travel she chooses	$50 to $75

In case you're wondering, I arrived at these price concessions by placing myself in the role of each buyer. You probably did the same thing as you went through each example. Don't be surprised if your price concessions differed from mine; we are, after all, individuals.

Using your personal price/value comparisons in the exercise above is fine, but you don't want to do that at work. For one thing, you may not be a low-price buyer for your company's offering. If you're not and you try to establish prices on the basis of *your* buying preferences, you'll offer larger price concessions than necessary. The result is that your company will leave money on the table with every sale it makes.

You want your customers and prospects to establish the value of each trade-off. They're the ones who'll be voting with their dollars. Focus groups and market surveys are two tools that can help you ascertain the values buyers place on the trade-offs you're asking them to make. That's how you assure that your company will be compensated well for the value it provides.

Let your buyers tell you what value they place on the trade-offs they're willing to make.

When targeting the low-cost buyer, make sure that you know:

1. Who your competitors are
2. What trade-offs your customers are willing to make
3. What value your customers place on each trade-off

Now that we have an approach for establishing prices for the low-cost buyer, let's do the same for the innovation buyer.

Innovation

People who are enthralled with new technology, new fashion or new services are willing to pay a high price to be on the cutting edge. To get a sense for how much they're willing to pay, let's look at a product that is nearing the end of its life, the VHS recorder.

In 1977, RCA introduced the first VHS VCR for $1,000. In the early 1990s, when many homes in the United States had more than one recorder, the price was around $250, 1/4 of the original offering price. Today, you can get a recorder for under $100, less than 1/10th it's original price.

The original price of an innovative offering will be 4 to 6 times its market acceptance price and 10 times its market maturity price.

The following graph shows this price/life cycle relationship.

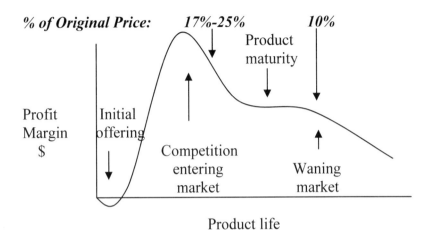

Figure 5.1 Product/profit margin life cycle

While it's nice to know how prices change over an innovative offering's life, it still doesn't answer the question, "How do you set the price for your latest invention?"

Common approach
Many business leaders, especially those involved in small and medium-sized businesses, set prices by taking the cost of the new product/service and adding the standard industry markup. Why? It's easier to estimate cost than predict buyer behavior. I didn't say it was a good reason, but that's the reason many companies revert to cost plus industry markup when pricing their innovations.

The price this calculation generates often gives management sticker shock; they can't believe that their customers will pay such a high price for their latest innovation. What do they do? They reexamine their cost estimates.

Eventually, these leaders realize that the price is high because the costs are expected to be high. Costs are expected to be high because demand and, consequently, production volumes are low in the early stages of a product/service's introduction. It's at this point that many leaders set the initial offering price at or slightly below their breakeven point. Why? To entice a lot of buyers quickly! The thought process goes like this.

A price at, or slightly below, breakeven will:

- Attract more buyers than a higher price
- Create familiarity with more buyers which speeds acceptance of the innovation
- Make the innovation profitable more quickly by allowing the innovator to experience economies of scale in its production efforts earlier than it could with higher prices
- Gain significant market share before competitors arrive with competing offerings

Makes sense, doesn't it? I'm not so sure. Let's reexamine the innovation buyers' profile.

Innovation buyers' profile
Innovation buyers:

- Love to be on the cutting edge
- Are willing to pay a lot of money for being first on the block to experience the latest, greatest invention

- Expect problems with these purchases, it's part of being on the leading edge
- Love regaling others with stories about the problems they've overcome

Take a moment to think about the people in your life. How many of them fit this profile? The answer I get most often is "less than 5%." That's a very small segment of the market.

Other buyers' profile
The question is, "Can you increase the number of innovation buyers by lowering your price?" Again, our VCR example offers some interesting insights.

If, in 1977, RCA had offered its VHS recorder for $800 instead of $1,000, how many more buyers would it have generated? We'll never know for sure, but it's likely the number would have been very small. Why? The answer lies in how most buyers respond to innovation. What do they do? They wait. The vast majority of buyers wait for:

- Assurance that the innovation isn't a fad
- The kinks to be eliminated
- The price to drop dramatically
- A clear understanding of the innovation's practicality
- Assurance that a better innovation isn't on the horizon

Are buyers with these interests likely to forego them for a lower price? Not likely! What's really going on here? By offering a lower price the seller is asking these buyers to make trade-offs that are contrary to their utilitarian natures. That's not comfortable for the buyer. If it's not comfortable, the buyer will wait.

As you can see, the belief that a low initial offering price will entice more buyers to an innovation is another of the great misconceptions about pricing. Don't fall into that trap.

Lower initial offering prices do not influence buyers' decisions regarding innovative products/services.

Since it's unlikely that lowering prices will significantly increase the number of innovation buyers, let's see whether higher prices are likely to drive innovation buyers away. For an answer to that question we'll return to our VCR example.

Higher initial offering price

Sony was "the first to market" with its Beta format, a higher quality format than VHS. Its initial offering price was $1,300. That's 30% higher than RCA's price of $1,000! Could RCA have gotten a similar price had it been first to market? Probably.

If VHS had been the only format available, innovation buyers would have had two options, pay the price or forego the experience. Based on your understanding of the innovation buyers' profile, which choice would they have made? Odds are they'd have paid the price.

For innovation buyers, the experience is more important than the price.

Knowing that high prices won't deter innovation buyers still doesn't answer the question, "Where do we set the price?" Again, I don't have a formula, only an approach that you can adapt to your company's situation.

Initial offering price

What should you charge for a new innovation? Here's a quick three-step process:

1. Estimate your production costs for the introduction stage. Yes, they'll be high; that's to be expected.
2. Calculate a price using a markup that's 50% higher than normal for your industry. If your industry's markup is 30%, make it 45%. The price calculated here represents the floor, the lowest initial price you'll charge for this offering.
3. Establish focus groups using only innovation buyers or survey these buyers to get their reaction to prices that are based on 100%, 150% and 200% of your industry's markup. Let their reactions guide you in establishing your initial offering price.

I'm sure that some of you are thinking, "That's obscene!" Is it? Your innovations bring them great joy; why shouldn't they reward you accordingly for your efforts? Remember, these profits also fuel the fire of future innovations, future enjoyment by these same buyers. Isn't that what you want? It's what they want.

Your initial offering price should include some multiple of your industry's typical markup. Let the innovation buyers tell you what that multiple should be.

We've got one more buying group to address, buyers who value customer intimacy. How do you price for these folks? Let's take a look.

Customer Intimacy

In order to provide an example similar to those provided for the low-cost and innovation buyers, I did an informal survey of retail operations. I chose Nordstrom, Famous-Barr (May Department Stores) and Penney's because these companies offer different levels of service.

Since my gender isn't noted for its shopping prowess, I limited my survey to the only frame of reference I have for judging price and quality, the men's department. Here are my findings:

Store	Quality	Service/Ambience	Price
Nordstrom	High quality, name brand merchandise	3 salespeople offered assistance within 20 minutes; all 3 graciously allowed me to browse; store was open, airy with a comforting piano accompaniment; attractive displays	2 to 3 times higher than Famous; 4 to 6 times higher than Penney's (some price difference relates to quality)
Famous-Barr	High quality, name brand merchandise	Saw one or two salespeople, no one approached, store seemed crowded with merchandise	Price was about twice that offered at Penney's
Penney's	Good quality, store brand merchandise	Did not see a salesperson; store crowded with merchandise	Significant discount to Nordstrom & Famous

As you can see, additional service and ambience can pay handsomely in higher prices. The key to knowing how much

of a premium to charge lies in knowing the demographics of
your buyers. In particular, you want to know what their
discretionary income is. Here are a couple of examples to
show how discretionary income influences the value placed
on service.

Low discretionary income
Years ago I played softball with a gentleman who worked as
a technician for a heating and air-conditioning contractor. He
made between $40,000 and $50,000 a year depending on how
much overtime he got. He also had 13 kids.

He and his wife were as happy as any couple I've ever known
despite the fact that discretionary income did not exist in their
household. At one of our games I overheard his wife telling
the other wives, "I buy whole chickens, I'm not about to pay
the butcher to cut them up for me." In essence, she was
saying that while she might enjoy that service, they didn't
have the discretionary income to pay for it.

High discretionary income
Now let's consider a working couple that makes a combined
salary of $80,000 a year. They each work about 50 hours per
week and they have no kids at home. This couple is likely to
pay for housekeeping service, eat out regularly and hire lawn
maintenance services. They have the discretionary income to
afford it.

> *Customer-intimate buyers typically have high levels of
> discretionary income.*

How much are customer-intimate buyers willing to pay for
great service? Again, I recommend that you use focus groups

and customer surveys to answer that question. You can, however, get a sense for what buyers are willing to pay by looking at their hourly rate of income. Here are a few examples to demonstrate this point.

A buyer who makes $8 an hour is likely to cut up whole chickens as the lady above did. She also does her own oil changes. It only takes a half-hour and a mechanic would charge $30, well beyond her hourly rate.

At $35 an hour the buyer's time becomes more valuable as do the services she hires. As her income approaches $100 per hour, there are many services she hires because "it's not worth her time to do it herself." That's human nature; it's the way we're built. Many buyers aren't even aware that they're making these choices. That's because the comparison of price and hourly income is being done subconsciously, just as all price/value comparisons are.

What does this mean for you and your company? It means that you need a clear picture of your buyer including her hourly rate of pay and discretionary income. If you don't have that information, you're likely to spend a lot of time and money marketing to people who are unwilling to buy.

Conversely, selling to customers whose discretionary income and hourly rate are high enough to view your service as a bargain will significantly increase the price you get and the profits you enjoy. That's what Nordstrom has done. It can work for your company too.

Note: *People, not businesses, make buying decisions. That's why these three buyer categories, low-cost, innovation and customer intimacy also apply to business-to-business sales.*

Other Misconceptions

At the beginning of this chapter I promised to discuss some of the "explanations" I get about why my clients "can't" raise prices. Here are their reasons:

- My competitors won't let me.
- I don't have the name awareness the big boys do.
- Competitor's customers won't talk to me unless I offer them lower prices.
- My goal is greater market share.
- The market is shrinking.

Let's explore each of these misconceptions in more detail.

Competition

I always ask new clients how their offerings differ from their competitors' offerings. Usually they spend anywhere from 45 minutes to an hour telling me why they're better than their competitors. Yet, when I ask them to raise prices, they cringe and tell me that "their competitors won't let them."

Does that make sense to you? It doesn't to me. If they're offering advantages their competitors don't, they should get higher prices for their offerings.

The only exception I can envision is when the "advantages" aren't valued by the buyer. In other words, these clients failed to ascertain the buyers' interests *before* creating their product/service. The obvious solution is to cut costs by eliminating the unwanted aspects of the offering.

You can charge a higher price than your competitors when customers value the advantages your offering affords.

The second "explanation" I get for not raising prices is that the client isn't as well known as her competitors.

Name Awareness

The owners of a residential builder client said they couldn't raise prices because they didn't have the name awareness of the well-established builders in the area. Is their reasoning valid or one more misconception? Let's see.

Assume that this builder's ad is running side by side with two well-established builders in his area. The homes are the same size, offer the same amenities and are located within 3 miles of one another. The price of my client's home is 10% lower than the other two builders. What would you think?

Did you suspect my client of offering lower quality than the other two builders? That's the conclusion they reached when I posed the scenario to them. Interestingly, they felt that they offered better quality than their competitors.

> *Name awareness should be created through marketing efforts, not pricing.*

The third "explanation" for low prices is that it's the only way to get your competitors' customers' business. Myth or reality; what do you think?

Attracting Competitors' Customers

There's no question that customers get comfortable with their suppliers. There are two factors that work against an outsider in situations like this:

1. Your competitor has rapport with the customer.
2. The fear of the unknown makes change difficult.

We've already discussed the value of rapport in Chapter 3, *Selling* and Chapter 4, *Customer Service*. I won't belabor the point here other than to say that rapport offers comfort and comfort is something that many people value.

The second factor, fear of the unknown, adds another layer of difficulty to getting your competitors' customers to give you a try. You know how that works. You know what it's like when you've got a trusted supplier and someone asks you to change. Let's be honest. Fear of the unknown often keeps us from making changes even when we're not entirely happy with our current situation, business or personal.

I'm not denying the challenge that's involved in getting your competitors' customers to give you a shot at their business. What I am saying is that there is a better way to attract them than lowering your prices.

A better way to open the door is to demonstrate value your competitors don't offer. That value might be higher quality, speedier delivery or additional services. The key to getting these buyers' attention is offering something they value that they aren't currently getting. That's what will open the door to your competitors' customers.

If you feel that the only way you'll get their attention is to offer lower prices, take a lesson from retailers. Make your low price a limited time offer. Here's the language retailers use when they offer lower prices:

- This weekend only
- Between 10:00 a.m. and noon
- While supply lasts

To get a sense for what happens when you don't use this language, place yourself in the role of the buyer. A seller approaches you with a lower price for one of your favorite products. Nothing is said about limits. What do you expect? Odds are you expect this low price on every purchase.

How will you feel if, within a month, the seller increases her price? How will you react? What's the likelihood she'll retain your business? Are you likely to shift your business back to your previous vendor? Why? The seller created an expectation that this low price would be in place for the foreseeable future, not just *one* month.

If you use low price to lure a competitor's customer, use this language. "I know that you need a reason to give us a shot at your business, so I'm going to offer you a discount on this order only. Once you've had a chance to experience the additional (quality, speed, service, etc.) we provide, the price will revert to its normal level of $\_\_\_$. I'm so certain that you'll be delighted with our (quality, speed, service, etc.) that I'm willing to offer this incentive on this order."

Now you've set the proper expectation. If that's not enough of an inducement, they're probably not a customer you want anyway. Move down the road to the next prospect.

If you use price as an inducement to a competitor's customer, use the language retailers use to limit the offer.

Many business leaders view lower prices as a tool for increasing market share. Is this a worthwhile business strategy or a prescription for failure?

Market Share

I haven't reviewed the seven deadly sins lately, but this has to be one of them. Let's face facts. There are only one or two companies that have the ability to garner significant market share in any industry. The best do it by providing what their customers can't get anywhere else. For low-cost buyers that means offering low prices, but for the majority of the buying public it means innovation or customer intimacy. Remember, Jay Conrad Levinson in his book, *Guerilla Marketing*,[14] said that most buyers do not consider price the determining factor in their buying decisions.

Companies that lower prices to gain market share often suffer heavy losses. They lose profit margin on each sale and their overhead grows to handle the additional volume. Since most buyers aren't swayed by lower prices alone, these companies often don't increase sales enough to cover the lost margin or additional overhead costs. That's a formula for failure.

Rather than go for market share, try gaining a competitive advantage that will earn your company premium prices. You won't work nearly so hard, but you'll be well-compensated.

> *Using low prices to gain market share often results in heavy losses and an opportunity for business failure.*

The final "explanation" for not raising prices is that the market is shrinking. Makes sense, doesn't it?

Shrinking Market

In every economy there are markets that are expanding, some that are stable and some that are shrinking. It's an inevitable

---

[14] Jay Conrad Levinson, *Guerilla Marketing*, Houghton Mifflin 1984

and endless progression. Why? Customer wants and needs are continuously changing.

If you find your company in a market that's shrinking, you may have to lower prices in the short run to buy time to find alternative markets. In situations like this, strong companies often use lower prices to drive weaker competitors out of business. You may be wondering whether this low-price strategy is cheaper than buying out your competitors. There is no hard, fast rule. Each situation must be evaluated on its own merits.

Well-run companies usually exit markets long before they begin to shrink. They often obsolete their own offerings. The leaders in these organizations know when the market's going to shrink; they're going to cause it to shrink.

Even when a company doesn't obsolete its own offerings, it can align itself closely with its customers. The more that's known about how customers' needs are changing, the easier it is to avoid being caught in a shrinking market.

Avoid shrinking markets with their attendant price declines. Anticipate your customers' changing needs. Better yet, obsolete your own offerings.

As you've just seen there are a lot of misconceptions about pricing. Let's make sure that in addressing them we haven't lost sight of the core concept. Then we'll explore some of the myths surrounding production in Chapter 6, *Production*.

Core Concept – Pricing

The goal of pricing is to be
compensated well for the value
you provide while giving greater
value than you receive.

Executive Summary – Pricing

- Raising prices is the quickest, least expensive way of increasing profits.

- We can categorize buyers by what they value most, low cost, innovation or customer intimacy.

- It's all about trade-offs. Buyers who want low prices are typically willing to forego innovation or service. Buyers who value innovation will forego low prices and service. Buyers seeking customer intimacy often forego the latest innovation and low prices to get the service they want.

- Low-cost buyers reward low price sellers.

- Innovation buyers typically pay prices 4 to 6 times the general market acceptance price and 10 times the market maturity price to get the latest, greatest innovation.

- Customer intimacy buyers weigh the services they want vs. their discretionary income and their hourly rate of pay.

PRODUCTION:

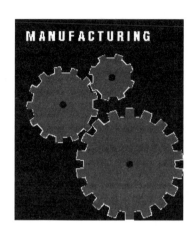

The endless search
for lower costs

6

Production

What is the goal of every successful production effort?

To provide the quality the customer wants, when he wants it, while continuously lowering production costs.

Core Concept – Lower Costs

Whether your company provides a product or service, your customers want what they want, when they want it, at the lowest possible price. Isn't that what we all want?

The key is lower costs. Theoretically, anyone can improve quality or shorten delivery times *if cost is no object*. I say theoretically because most of us have been disappointed by poor quality and late deliveries despite having paid a hefty price. Companies that accomplish all three, better quality, timely delivery and low costs, gain:

- The ability to charge premium prices; you can get premium pricing when you offer superior quality and/or speed of delivery
- Higher profit margins; the result of premium pricing and low costs
- Strong customer loyalty; happy customers usually become repeat customers
- Greater ability to thrive during price wars; low costs allow them to remain profitable while cutting prices

These are significant advantages. How do you gain them? To answer that question we need to explore each of the three elements of production. Let's begin with quality.

Quality

What is quality? It depends on whom you ask. Customers and producers typically have different answers. I use the term "producer" purposely to reflect the fact that the concepts in this chapter apply equally well to products and services. Now let's see how customers and producers view quality.

As consumers we define quality in terms of dependability, repair costs, aesthetics or functionality. Producers define quality by number of errors, cost of rework or amount of scrap generated.

The consumer's definition identifies what he values while the producer's definition quantifies mistakes. Both influence your company's production costs, but in very different ways. We'll begin with the consumer's definition.

Customer's perspective on quality

A printer taught me to view quality through the customer's eyes. We were discussing quality's influence on pricing when he asked, "When a customer walks through my door which do you think he's more likely to buy, a good print job or a great print job?" "A great job!", I replied.

He gave me one of those *Gotcha!* grins and said "Most people can't tell the difference between a good print job and great print job, yet the cost of a great print job is dramatically higher." His message was clear. The consumer is only going to pay for the quality he can see.

Has your company added bells, whistles, glitz and glamour to your offerings? If so, are they valued by your customers? Not sure! Here are a few questions to help you determine whether the customer values your "improvements."

1. Has the profit margin improved on your offering since the improvements?
2. Has your market share increased even though you've raised your prices to cover the improvements?
3. Are you experiencing more referrals from existing customers as a result of these improvements?

If your answers are "No" or "I'm not sure", your company could be adding significant cost to its offerings without gaining any advantage. Think about it. Every feature you build into your offering adds cost. If the customer doesn't see how that feature is going to help him, he's not going to pay extra for it.

Some of you may be thinking, "But these bells and whistles differentiate our offerings from our competitors' offerings."

Do they really? Do you really think that a buyer is more likely to buy your offerings because it includes unwanted features? Would you? Allow me to ask that another way. What do you do when salespeople emphasize features that don't interest you? Do you

1. Factor them into your decision?
2. Discard them as irrelevant?
3. Walk away frustrated because the salesperson isn't listening to you?

Let me guess. #3?

Remember what we learned in Chapter 1, *Strategy*. The way to differentiate your offerings from competitors' offerings is to provide something the market *wants or needs* that it isn't getting. If you're not gaining the advantages outlined in the three questions above, odds are you're offering something the market doesn't want.

Providing "improvements" that your customers don't value usually translates into higher costs and lower margins.

We'll deal with the producer's definition of quality when we discuss methods for lowering costs. For now let's turn our attention to timely delivery.

Timely Delivery
That's it; that's the snowboard you've always wanted! You race to the counter, credit card in hand, grinning ear to ear. What's that? They're on backorder and the display model is damaged. This store has been waiting for a shipment for two months and the producer still won't commit to a delivery date. What do you do?

It depends on how badly you want that particular board. If it's the only board that will satisfy you, you'll wait. You'll resent it, but you'll wait. When the board arrives, what will you feel, joy or relief? Will you be happy that you've finally got the board or relieved that the wait is over?

Then there's the possibility that when the board arrives it's flawed. What do you do then? Wait several more months or live with the imperfection?

Is it fair to say that regardless of whether the board arrives flawed or in mint condition, your enjoyment is diminished because you had to wait for delivery?

Your only alternative, assuming you just have to have a new snowboard, is to buy a competitor's board. It may not be the board of your dreams, but you can enjoy it *immediately*.

How does this affect the producer? The best he can hope to achieve is a dissatisfied customer, you. At worst, he loses your business to a competitor. Either way, his reputation takes another hit every time you recount your experience. That's a high price to pay for late delivery.

Alternatives
Companies that understand these consequences often resort to extraordinary measures to avoid being late. They expedite orders in their plants or they ship "next day delivery." Both of these alternatives are expensive. Let's see how expensive they can be.

Expedited orders
Expediting orders disrupts production flow, increases the number of errors and slows production of remaining orders.

That's true whether you're offering a product or service. Here's what happens.

You're asked to stop what you're doing, expedite an order then return to your original task. This shifting back and forth causes you to reorient yourself twice. Each time you reorient yourself, you lose time. It cannot be recovered.

Reorientations also invite mistakes. The more often you are asked to make these mental shifts, the more likely you are to miss something during a reorientation. Voila, more mistakes!

Expediting orders often begets more expediting. Companies typically don't add more people or equipment to expedite orders. That means employees are expected to complete both their scheduled production and the expedited orders. How likely is that? This folly creates an ever-increasing backlog of late orders which require expediting.

As you can imagine companies that regularly expedite orders experience soaring production costs without an attendant growth in revenue. In fact, these companies often experience revenue declines because they aren't delivering on time. A company which is habitually late with its deliveries invites its competitors into its customers' offices opening the door to further revenue loss. Now, there's a formula for failure.

Expediting orders, while usually viewed as a temporary fix, often results in permanent, costly system inefficiencies.

An alternative to expediting orders is speeding delivery. Some companies opt to use next day delivery in lieu of expediting orders in the production department. What does that cost? Let's see.

Next day delivery

Let's assume that you are the producer. Due to a production problem you're going to miss a customer's deadline unless you use next day delivery. What's the likelihood that you'll recover those costs? Does the phrase, slim to none, come to mind? As a buyer, would you absorb these costs?

If you want to estimate these costs for your company

1. Subtract your normal delivery cost from the next day delivery cost;
2. Multiply this difference by the number of next day delivery orders precipitated by production problems.

Next day delivery is another temporary fix that often results in costly system inefficiencies.

How do you avoid these costs? Address the causes of your production delays! Remove these problems! Then you'll only use next day delivery when your customers request it.

Adding bells and whistles that your customers don't value and scrambling to meet delivery deadlines are both costly propositions. They make it difficult to achieve the third aspect of the core concept, continuously declining costs.

Continuously Declining Costs

There are a number of excellent approaches available to you if you are truly committed to this goal. I'm going to provide a brief overview of each of them, then refer you to books that provide a more detailed treatment of the subject. There's no point in reiterating what's been so skillfully written by others.

The approaches we'll be discussing are:

- Benchmarking
- Reengineering
- Activity-Based Management
- Six Sigma
- Lean Manufacturing
- Theory of Constraints

Benchmarking

Benchmarking is a technique for learning from the best. You find a group, department or organization that's noted for their ability to accomplish a lot with few resources. Observe their system. Then adopt those practices that are superior to yours. As your group's productivity rises, your costs drop.

While companies often benchmark themselves against non-competing companies, that's not necessary. It's not unusual for one division or plant to excel at production and struggle with sales. One may have good employee relations and be technologically inept while another may have the opposite experience. Benchmarking can help you lower costs and increase profits by disseminating your company's best practices throughout your organization.

When do you need to go outside your organization? Here's the short list; it's certainly not exhaustive.

- Your group is the best in your organization.
- Many people in your organization suffer from the "it can't be good unless it was invented here" syndrome.
- You don't have comparable processes in other areas of your operation.

Companies that allow others to benchmark them often require requesting companies to do some homework first. There are two reasons for that.

1. Benchmark companies want to make sure that the requesting firm is committed to the effort.
2. Benchmark firms don't want to use their employees' time to educate the requesting firm's staff about the basics of benchmarking.

Benchmarking enables your company to lower costs by learning from the best.

Note: While this chapter focuses on production costs, benchmarking can be used to reduce costs in any process. It's been used to reduce check processing costs in finance departments, hiring costs in human resource functions and call-handling costs in customer service departments. These costs also need to be recouped in your selling price. The more you reduce these ancillary costs, the more profitable your company becomes.

Benchmarking is a powerful tool. It does require an open mind. You cannot learn from others if you think you have all the answers. Even if your group is one of the most efficient at what it does, it can always be better. To deny that is to say that you've achieved perfection. I doubt that you're willing to make that claim.

If benchmarking doesn't fit your style, maybe our second approach, reengineering, will interest you.

Reengineering
In their book, *Reengineering the Corporation,*[15] Michael
Hammer and James Champy challenge business leaders to
quit tinkering with existing processes. Instead, they suggest
that they create new processes based on the circumstances
and technologies that exist *today.*

While the idea is sound, reengineering resulted in a number
of significant failures in the 1990's. Why? As the authors
admitted, they forgot the people. They didn't give enough
consideration to reengineering's impact on the workforce.

In addition, there were three flaws in the way reengineering
was implemented in these failed efforts.

1. Many external consultants involved in implementing
   reengineering arrived on the scene sporting the
   "expert" mentality. Consequently, the client's
   employees weren't involved in designing new
   processes. Shame on my profession.
2. Many external consultants "sold" reengineering as a
   way to reduce head count. Shame on my profession.
3. Leaders in client organizations were more interested
   in reducing headcount than finding ways to use the
   time, talents and energy of their people to achieve
   greater profits. Shame on them.

Is it any wonder that employees' survival instincts were
triggered in these organizations? Can you imagine their
reticence when their work processes were being evaluated?

---

[15] Michael Hammer & James Champy, *Reengineering the Corporation: A
Manifesto for Business Revolution*, HarperBusiness, 1993

The final affront comes when employees are told that their way of doing things is inefficient. Can you imagine how badly these employees want to prove the "experts" wrong?

Don't let the mistakes made in the early 1990s dissuade you from using this tool. Reengineering allows you and your staff to dream, to explore the realm of the possible without the hindrance of what exists.

Use customers' needs to guide you in designing processes. Explore new technologies to see how they might help you meet those needs. It's the kind of thinking that often results in performance breakthroughs and lower costs. It's not easy, but then is anything worthwhile accomplished with ease?

Reengineering challenges you to reduce costs
by utilizing today's technology to design new processes
to satisfy your customer's needs.

Cost reduction approach #3, activity-based management, was originally called activity-based costing. Let's see how it can help us reduce costs.

Activity-Based Management (ABM)
ABM says that gross profit (sales minus production costs) is not a reliable measure of a product's/service's profitability. Why? Gross profit doesn't consider marketing, procurement or service costs. For example, the cost of purchasing raw materials for Product A might be significantly higher than for Product B because:

- Product A has more components
- Product A's components are more difficult to obtain
- Product A's components require longer lead times and more follow up

As you can see, procurement costs can vary widely by product, yet they typically aren't included in the gross profit calculation. Even if they are, their inclusion is accomplished through some nebulous allocation formula. The following example will demonstrate this point.

Under traditional cost accounting the cost of acquiring the raw materials is often allocated on the basis of unit volume produced. Let's say that a company produces 12,000 units per month, 3,000 units of Product A and 9,000 units of Product B. If this company allocates procurement costs, it's likely to allocate 25% (3,000 units/12,000 units) to Product A and 75% (9,000 units/12,000 units) to Product B.

At the top of this page we listed several factors that influence procurement costs. Does this formula make sense in light of these factors? If not, you're embracing ABM's philosophy.

ABM says that output has little, if any, bearing on the ease or difficulty in acquiring raw materials. Instead ABM maps the processes used in acquiring raw materials for each product. Then it identifies the costs associated with each step in the process. The total procurement cost for a product is simply the sum of the costs identified in the process steps.

Total procurement cost helps us allocate the purchasing department's costs. Allocations are made by multiplying the product's total procurement cost times the number of raw material orders placed for that product. Doesn't that make more sense than allocating these costs on the basis of output?

ABM's alpha omega approach

Proponents of ABM suggest that the best way to evaluate a product's/service's profitability is by applying the ABM approach to the entire business process, marketing, sales, order processing, purchasing, production, quality control, shipping, invoicing, collection and accounting. ABM is designed to provide an overall evaluation of the profitability of each product/service your company offers.

A natural byproduct of ABM analysis is the discovery of system inefficiencies. Since ABM involves quantifying the cost of each step in the process, you'll also discover the cost of these inefficiencies. The rest is easy:

1. List each inefficiency
2. Develop a plan for removing the inefficiency
3. Prioritize your action items based on the magnitude of cost savings

The result is a cost reduction plan that allows you to achieve dramatic cost savings quickly.

Activity-Based Management is designed to provide a clearer picture of each offering's profitability while uncovering cost reduction opportunities.

The next cost reduction approach we're going to explore is Six Sigma. It's been popular with Fortune 500 companies; can it work for you? Let's see.

Six Sigma

Six Sigma's espoused goal is to reduce costs while increasing customer satisfaction. Bravo! It's refreshing to see a cost reduction approach that considers the customer.

Cost reduction is accomplished by removing *opportunities* for mistakes in both the production and service aspects of your company's offerings. Six Sigma gets its name from a statistical measure which indicates an error rate of three defects per million. The Six Sigma approach evaluates processes, identifies opportunities for error and removes those opportunities. For those of you who feel that three defects per million is an unrealistic goal, let me remind you that dogged determination when combined with lofty goals often produces exceptional results *even if* the target isn't hit.

Six Sigma involves extensive training for a select group of your company's employees. These employees are educated in process evaluation and statistical analysis. Once they've successfully completed their studies, they're given the title, "black belt." Each black belt is assigned to a team which spends the next couple of years employing its skills in cost reduction/customer satisfaction activities.

You're probably wondering, "Do these black belts use the same techniques to accomplish both cost reduction and enhanced customer satisfaction?" The answer is, "Yes," but where they focus their attention can be dramatically different. Let's see how they tackle cost reduction.

Cost reduction

If the black belt team's focus is on reducing errors and the attendant frustration they cause your customers, they'll focus on costs. Which costs? Typically scrap and rework costs.

Both of these costs result from errors (system inefficiencies). That's where the black belts usually start.

During their process examinations, black belts often uncover "hidden factories," stages in the process where mistakes are routinely caught and fixed (reworked) *before* production is complete. Hidden factories arise in response to mandated error limits measured at the *end* of the production process rather than at each stage of the process. In essence, workers create hidden factories to meet management's expectations.

You can imagine how quickly hidden factories become imbedded in the production system, how transparent they are to management and how expensive they can be. Black belts eliminate hidden factories by requiring error measurement *at each stage of the process*.

Six Sigma produces cost savings by reducing opportunities for errors and eliminating hidden factories.

How does this cost reduction approach differ from the customer satisfaction approach? That's what we're going to explore next.

Customer satisfaction
When black belts focus on customer satisfaction they ask themselves, "How well is our production process aligned with our customers' wishes?" What does that mean?

The story about a printer that I related in Chapter 5, *Pricing*, will illustrate this point. The printer taught me that most people aren't willing to pay for a great print job. Why? Two reasons:

1. They can't see the difference between a good job and a great job.
2. The cost of a great print job is dramatically higher than the cost of a good print job.

In this instance, black belts would assure that the printer wasn't providing great print jobs when his customers were only willing to pay for a good print job. That's the alignment Six Sigma is seeking.

Production processes that are aligned to customers' wishes produce only what the customer values, nothing more. This alignment keeps unnecessary costs out of the system and speeds delivery to the customer. Everyone wins! Customers get what they want quickly. The company reduces its costs and earns greater customer loyalty. I love multiple benefits from the same effort, don't you?

Six Sigma reduces costs by making sure that the company's production efforts are aligned with customers' wishes.

While it affords tremendous benefits, Six Sigma isn't for everyone. The training fees are hefty and your organization has to employ enough people for you to be able to pull some of them off their jobs for up to two years. Many companies simply don't have the resources to employ Six Sigma.

The two remaining cost reduction approaches, Lean Manufacturing and Theory of Constraints, attack the same misconception, so I'm combining them into one section.

Lean Manufacturing/Theory of Constraints
Like ABM, Lean Manufacturing and Theory of Constraints blame traditional cost accounting for system inefficiencies.

We've already discussed Activity Based Management. You know that it's designed to:

- Measure each offering's profitability more accurately by including the marketing, selling, order processing, quality control, shipping, invoicing, collection and accounting costs in the analysis
- Identify and eliminate system inefficiencies to increase the profitability of each offering

ABM criticizes traditional cost accounting for only including production costs when calculating a product's/service's profits. ABM advocates argue that all of the costs in the first bullet point above should be included in the calculation.

Proponents of Lean Manufacturing and Theory of Constraints challenge a different aspect of cost accounting, the concept of unit cost. They say that business leaders often labor under the misconception that low unit costs are only attainable with large batch runs. Let's see whether they're right.

Cost – traditional cost accounting
Traditional cost accounting focuses on cost per unit *for each stage of production*. To get a sense for how this works, let's assume that there are three stages in your production process, A, B and C.

The maximum number of units that can be produced in each stage are as follows:

	Units/hour
Stage A	30
Stage B	50
Stage C	10

The combined costs including raw materials, labor, fringes, equipment, facility costs, supervision and quality control are:

	Cost/hour
Stage A	$15
Stage B	$50
Stage C	$90

The table below shows how traditional cost accounting calculates unit cost for various levels of production.

Stage	A	B	C
Cost/hour	$15	$50	$90
Unit cost for 2 units/hour	$7.50	$25.00	$45.00
Unit cost for 5 units/hour	$3.00	$10.00	$18.00
Unit cost for 10 units/hour	$1.50	$ 5.00	$ 9.00

You can see how dramatically unit costs drop as unit volume increases. The natural conclusion is that we ought to produce as many units as we can at each stage of production to bring our unit costs down. In this example, A would produce 30 units/hour, B would also produce 30 units/hour since it relies on A's production and A can only produce 30 units/hour, C produces 10 units/hour, its maximum. The production rates and unit costs are shown in the table below:

Stage	A	B	C
Units/hour	30	30	10
Cost/unit	$.50	$1.67	$9.00

In this example the total unit cost is $11.17 ($.50 +$1.67+ $9.00 = $11.17).

Traditional cost accounting measures unit cost by calculating the unit cost for each stage of production.

Let's see how that differs from the Lean Manufacturing and Theory of Constraints approaches.

Cost – Lean Manufacturing/Theory of Constraints

Lean Manufacturing and Theory of Constraints argue that traditional cost accounting overlooks an expensive reality; inventory is building in Stage C. The following table is designed to help you visualize what's happening. Inventory for each stage is calculated using the following formula:

Units received from the previous department
(for A that's the materials store)
- Units completed and transferred out
+ Beginning inventory
= Ending inventory

	A's inventory	B's inventory	C's inventory
End of hour 1	30-30+0= 0	30-30+0= 0	30-10+ 0= 20
End of hour 2	30-30+0= 0	30-30+0= 0	30-10+20= 40
End of hour 3	30-30+0= 0	30-30+0= 0	30-10+40= 60

Neither A nor B experience any inventory buildup because they're both operating at or under capacity. C is building inventory at the rate of 20 units per hour because its capacity is lower than B's. This inventory impacts the company in a couple of ways. First, it ties up the company's cash. Second, inventory increases the company's operating costs.

The table below shows us how much cash is being tied up in Stage C inventory. We'll use the traditional cost accounting unit costs of $.50 for A ($15/hour divided by 30 units), $1.67 for B ($50/hour divided by 30 units produced). We don't include C's unit cost in the calculation because C has not performed any work on the inventory. The formula is:

(A's unit cost + B's unit cost) x # of units added to inventory

	Increase in inventory	Total inventory
Hour 1	(.50+1.67) x 20 = 43.40	43.40
Hour 2	(.50+1.67) x 20 = 43.40	86.80
Hour 3	(.50+1.67) x 20 = 43.40	130.20

That's $347 a day; $1,736 a week; $7,634 per month. This is one small production process with relatively low volumes. Can you imagine how much money large companies tie up in inventory when they use traditional cost accounting's unit cost approach?

At this point, we've only calculated the cost of the inventory. We still have to consider the handling, storage, tracking, insurance and financing costs involved with maintaining inventory. If that isn't enough, there are several other risks looming on the horizon:

- Loss due to accident, theft or shelf-life expiration
- A change in customer preferences that makes the inventory obsolete
- Entrance of competitors with more attractive offerings, again, making the inventory obsolete
- Technological obsolescence

Obviously, Lean Manufacturing and Theory of Constraint arguments are valid. The question is, "What do you do if you find your company in this situation?" Here's what these two approaches suggest:

- Ignore your equipment's capacity; base your production runs on customer demand
- Stop producing in areas where you have significant inventory; you'll free up a lot of cash quickly
- Reevaluate your equipment; use customer demand rather than unit cost to drive your equipment investment decisions
- Replace equipment that has excess capacity as soon as possible; remember, it's easier to take medicine in one gulp than it is to sip it

Both Lean Manufacturing and Theory of Constraints admit that while their inventory reduction strategies generate a lot of cash, they often have a negative impact on profits. It's an accounting quirk that is described in both *The Goal*[16] (Theory of Constraints) and *Lean Thinking*[17] (Lean Manufacturing) so I won't rehash it here.

I will say that the prospect of lower profits tends to influence managers of publicly-traded companies more than it does owners of privately-held companies. Managers in publicly-traded companies are typically rewarded for current profits, not long-term profitability.

---

[16] Eliyahu Goldratt, *The Goal*, The North River Press, 1984, 1986, 1992
[17] James Womack & Daniel Jones, *Lean Thinking*, Simon & Schuster, 1996

Conversely, business owners are rewarded for creating value. Their reward comes when they sell the business. That's why they tend to have a longer-term perspective than managers of publicly-traded companies.

While Lean Manufacturing and Theory of Constraints attack the same misconception and have similar goals, they vary in the way they approach the problem.

Lean Manufacturing vs. Theory of Constraints
The primary difference I see between Theory of Constraints and Lean Manufacturing is that Lean Manufacturing focuses heavily on equipment placement and work area layout as a way to remove waste. Lean Manufacturing continuously reviews production flows and repositions equipment on the basis of its findings. While equipment placement may change in the Theory of Constraints approach, it isn't touted as an integral part of the approach itself.

Theory of Constraints identifies the weak link in the chain and strengthens it. Then it looks for the new weak link. This process is repeated endlessly. That's Theory of Constraints' approach to continuously lowering costs.

Another distinction between Lean Manufacturing and Theory of Constraints is that Lean Manufacturing and Six Sigma are being used in tandem. It's too early to judge the benefits of this combination, but intuitively it makes sense.

Both Six Sigma and Lean Manufacturing have goals of reducing production costs and aligning production with customer desires. Six Sigma lacks the equipment placement techniques of Lean Manufacturing. Lean Manufacturing is missing the statistical analysis tools of Six Sigma. Time will tell, but this combination looks promising. Again, the benefits are more likely to be achieved by large companies.

Another distinction between Lean Manufacturing and Theory of Constraints is that Theory of Constraints can been applied to service businesses. To demonstrate this point Eliyahu Goldratt wrote *Necessary But Not Sufficient*[18] in which he applies his Theory of Constraints to a software firm.

If I were asked to choose between Lean Manufacturing and Theory of Constraints, I'd suggest Theory of Constraints to most companies. It doesn't have the technical requirements of Lean Manufacturing or Six Sigma for that matter. It's also easier for most business leaders to employ because there's an intuitive nature to it.

Lean Manufacturing focuses heavily on equipment placement and work area layout.

Theory of Constraints identifies the weak link in the chain, strengthens it, then looks for the new weak link. This approach works equally in product and service businesses.

This completes our quick and dirty review of some of the more successful cost reduction approaches available today. If you are interested in learning more about any of these topics, here's a brief bibliography to help in your quest.

Benchmarking For Best Practices
Christopher E. Bogan and Michael J. English
McGraw-Hill 1994

---

[18] Eliyahu Goldratt, *Necessary But Not Sufficient*, The North River Press, 2000

Reengineering the Corporation
Michael Hammer and James Champy
HarperBusiness 1993

Implementing Activity-Based Cost Management
Robin Cooper, Robert S. Kaplan, Lawrence S. Maisel,
Eileen Morrissey and Ronald M. Oehm
Institute of Management Accountants 1992

The Six Sigma Way
Peter Pande, Robert Neuman, Roland Cavanagh
McGraw-Hill 2000

Lean Six Sigma
Michael L. George
McGraw-Hill 2002

Lean Thinking
James P. Womack and Daniel T. Jones
Simon & Schuster 1996

The Goal
Eliyahu M. Goldratt
The North River Press 1984, 1986, 1992

Necessary But Not Sufficient
Eliyahu M. Goldratt
The North River Press 2000

It's time to turn our attention to other misconceptions that
thwart a company's ability to "continuously lower costs."

Other Misconceptions

Here are some things organizations overlook when trying to lower costs:

- Their organization's desire to reduce costs
- A long-term perspective
- The sustainability of process improvements
- The need to continuously monitor customer desires

I can see you smiling. You're way ahead of me on this one, aren't you? You know that very few companies demonstrate an interest in, much less a talent for incorporating these elements in their cost reduction strategies. To understand why, let's explore each of these elements in more detail.

Desire

Many companies talk about reducing costs, but how many work diligently at it? In *Lean Thinking*, Womack and Jones, state that managements of most companies won't initiate cost reduction efforts unless they're experiencing a great deal of pain. That's been my experience as well.

The obvious question is, "Why?" Some of the explanations you're likely to hear are:

- We're creatures of habit
- We don't like change
- We're too busy
- We don't have the right leadership
- We're doing very well, thank you very much

As lame as these excuses are, they reflect the reality that exists in corporate America today. How do you overcome

this resistance to cost reduction? People skilled in neuro-
linguistic programming, the study of the impact of language
on human behavior, would say that we're using the wrong
language. They would suggest that instead of establishing a
goal of cutting costs, you set a goal of having competitors
ask, "How do they do that?" I'm sure you can feel the
difference the language makes. Let's explore the psychology
that creates this feeling.

When you ask employees to cut costs, they feel that they're
being asked to forego something they want. It doesn't matter
that your goal is to help them become more successful; all
they hear is that you want them to give something up.

Conversely, when you ask employees to help you become the
envy of your competitors, they see themselves as contributors
in an organization that's admired by competitors, if not the
entire business community. They imagine the pride they'll
feel as others learn of their employment at a company with a
stellar reputation. Employees know that greatness will be
attributed to them by virtue of their employment. Which of
these two approaches do you think is more likely to engage
your employees?

Interestingly, companies that outperform their competitors
experience lower costs. "Outperform" means accomplishing
more with fewer resources. Since every resource has a cost,
the fewer resources you use the lower your costs become.
How can you make this work in your organization? Here's
how one business did it.

A neuro-linguistically sound message
A Pizza Hut delivery location near my home has a white
board above the counter. On that board they listed their goal,

"100% on-time deliveries, every week, without an accident."
Along side the goal was the percentage for the current week
and the number of consecutive weeks without an accident.

All of the outcomes listed in this goal are positive. The goal
itself is easy to embrace because it is good for the customers,
the employees and the franchise. It's obvious that on-time
deliveries make the customer happy. It's equally obvious
that employees don't want to be involved in accidents, but
does the franchise owner gain from this goal? Here are a few
of the benefits he gains:

1. The franchisee doesn't pay for complimentary pizzas
    or drinks in hope of salvaging an unhappy customer.
2. Timely deliveries earn repeat business which reduces
    marketing costs. I have yet to see a study that shows
    that it's cheaper to get orders from new customers
    than from existing ones.
3. Fewer accidents means lower insurance premiums for
    both workman's compensation insurance and general
    liability insurance.
4. Employee turnover drops as employees come to trust
    that the franchisee has their welfare at heart. Low
    turnover produces savings in three ways: lower hiring
    costs, lower training costs and fewer mistakes.

These are significant savings, yet cost savings was never
mentioned in the goal.

Imagine how you'd feel if you were an employee of this
franchise and the stated goal had been to "reduce insurance
costs by 15% through fewer accidents." Could you get
excited about this goal? Why not?

The goal implies only one interest, reducing insurance costs. It doesn't speak to your welfare as an employee or to the customer's desire for timely delivery. Is that any different than business leaders asking employees to cut costs?

If you want to create desire for cost reduction initiatives, establish goals that inspire your workers to greatness and consider their needs.

Desire isn't the only thing missing in many cost reduction strategies; the long-term perspective is absent as well.

Long-Term Perspective

In the United States we demand instant gratification. That's reflected in our compensation programs. We'll pay for results, but we want those results *now*. This attitude flies in the face of production's goal of *continuously* lower costs. All of the approaches we discussed share a common theme; cost reduction is an ongoing process, not an occasional project. How do you develop a long-term perspective?

First, you get comfortable with the idea that no matter how proficient you become at lowering costs, you'll never be perfect. There will always be a more cost effective way to produce your offerings.

Some of you may find that discouraging; I find it refreshing. Think about it. Imagine what it would be like to get up in the morning knowing that you'll never be any better off than you were yesterday. Would you even bother getting up?

Remind your employees that greatness is a lifelong pursuit and success is simply movement toward your next goal.

Many companies that use cost reduction strategies experience what I call "the seesaw effect." Employees and leaders work diligently to reduce costs only to see them rise again. Why does that happen? How can you avoid having this happen to your company? That's the topic of our next section.

Sustainability

Unfortunately, the benefits of many costs reduction efforts are lost in a very short time. Why? Here are a few reasons:

- Employee resistance
- Changes in management
- The flavor-of-the-month approach to management
- The relentless cycle of hiring and downsizing

Employee resistance

A former chairman of Porsche admonished his audience to "Decide democratically, delegate dictatorially." What does it mean to decide democratically? It means that you involve your employees in deciding what needs to change and how to effect that change. It's only when they have a vested interest in the change that they embrace it, work through the difficult times and sustain the results accomplished.

If you force change upon them, they'll resist. If the change feels threatening they may even sabotage the effort. I'm not condoning this behavior; I'm merely acknowledging the fact that survival is a powerful motivator.

Involving employees in change initiatives is easier in smaller organizations than in large ones. When you can't involve all of your employees, set up mechanisms that allow those not involved to offer suggestions. Recognize and reward those whose suggestions you use. Thank those who took the time to offer suggestions even though they're not used. These simple actions allow your employees to feel involved even though they're not part of the planning team.

Once a plan is devised and consensus achieved, delegate dictatorially. Assign tasks; establish expectations; set deadlines. Your employees expect you to take control at this point. Don't disappoint them.

Porsche's former chairman offered another perspective on "Decide democratically, delegate dictatorially" when he said, "A poor idea implemented well produces better results than a good idea implemented poorly." In other words, when your employees embrace an idea, they'll make it successful; if they don't like it, the results will be marginal.

A poor idea implemented well produces better results than a good idea implemented poorly.

If you want your cost reduction efforts to produce long-term results, involve your employees. Otherwise, your savings will be fleeting (but you get to enjoy the seesaw).

The tenure of senior executives, whether in a plant, division or the corporation itself, is rapidly approaching the lifespan of a mayfly. It's like a revolving door in corporate America. It's also one of the reasons why it's so difficult to sustain the results of cost reduction efforts.

Management changes
Each change in management seems to bring a change in direction. Why is that? You need look no further than your own motivations to answer this question.

Let's say that you just received a promotion. What do you want to accomplish more than anything else? Be honest! Aren't you interested in proving that your superiors made the right decision?

The impetus for change that accompanies virtually every management change is the desire of the manager to make a name for himself. The easiest way to do that is to scrap the old regime's model and install a new one. Scrapping earlier cost reduction strategies in favor of new ones often results in the loss of earlier benefits. That's why cost reductions don't often survive management changes.

If you've recently taken a new leadership position, beware! The natural tendency is to try to make a name for yourself quickly. Resist this temptation. Evaluate existing systems *before* making changes. Distinguish yourself by salvaging much of the current savings while finding ways to increase those savings.

Resist the temptation to scrap the old regime's model. While there may be times when that's appropriate, more often than not, the old model simply needs tuning.

Even when a company doesn't make frequent management changes, it can experience the savings losses just described. This occurs when its leaders fall victim to the "flavor of the month" management style.

Flavor of the month
Mid-level managers in virtually every organization with which I've dealt bemoan senior leaderships' reading lists. To them it seems that every time a new idea appears on the horizon, they're shifting gears and moving another direction.

In many cases, they're right. Direction is changed so often that these organizations experience the cost, but seldom the benefits, of new initiatives. This is contrary to the stated production goal of continuously lowering production costs. How do you avoid this dilemma?

If you're a member of senior management, ask yourself, "Does this concept fit our plan?" If you're operating below that level, be prepared to demonstrate the benefits the current initiative is producing. Then ask senior management, "How does the potential savings of the new cost reduction approach compare to the future savings from our current initiative?"

Some of you are thinking, "If I attempted that with my boss, I'd be looking for another job." If that's the case, you may want to look for one anyway. The environment you're in isn't conducive to your personal or career growth.

> *Be open to new ideas, but don't adopt them blindly.*
> *Ask yourself, "How does this fit into our plan?"*

One of the greatest obstacles to sustaining cost savings is the seemingly endless cycle of hiring and downsizing. Let's see what impact this cycle has.

Hiring/downsizing
We've already discussed the importance of involving your employees in cost reduction decisions. All too often the people who produce these savings are later swept away in the tide of short-term profit management called downsizing. When they leave, the organization loses:

- Knowledge of why processes were changed
- What benefits those changes were producing
- An understanding of how processes were to evolve to achieve even more cost reductions

Often the survivors of a downsizing are forced to redesign processes in an attempt to cope with an unconscionable work load. These process redesigns have one goal, expediency. Cost-savings isn't even a consideration.

In this chapter we've discussed some truly amazing tools:

- Benchmarking
- Reengineering
- Activity-Based Management
- Six Sigma
- Lean Manufacturing
- Theory of Constraints

I've often wondered why senior managers don't require operating managers to use these tools to verify the need for additional staffing. Experience has taught me that it's easy to effect a 20% improvement in productivity even in well-run operations. That means much of the hiring that's done is unnecessary. Indiscriminate hiring leads to overstaffing and the inevitable need for downsizing. This can be avoided by using the tools in this chapter *without* investing a great deal of time.

I'd be surprised if you didn't have some doubts. Let me share an experience with you. On a recent visit to one of my clients, the operations manager announced that he needed five more people. When I asked why, he laid out his plan in great detail. It was a good plan, but I doubted that he needed five people to implement it.

I suggested that we take a few minutes and reexamine the strengths of the people he already employed, the work they were doing and contrast the benefits of what they were doing against the benefits his plan offered. In less than an hour, we found that he could accomplish everything he desired with one new person. He didn't need five.

Why did this happen? The operations manager knew that all of his employees were busy. He trusted their judgment. That's why he felt that he had to add five more people to implement his plan. He never considered the possibility that some of the things his employees were doing had little, if any, value. He failed to realize that, as human beings, we're all creatures of habit; that we do things because we've always done them. These oversights caused him to overlook ways of accomplishing his goal without adding staff.

You can see how easy it is for a manager to overestimate his staffing needs. You can get a sense for the magnitude of this problem through a simple calculation. Assume that every manager in your organization is employing at least one more person than he needs. How many operating managers do you have? That's a reasonable estimate of the overstaffing that exists in your organization.

You know me well enough by now to know that I'm not suggesting that you cut staff to rectify this overstaffing. Instead, focus your attention on growing revenues *without* adding staff. You can quickly absorb this "overstaffing" through higher revenues.

Remember it takes years to realize the full benefit of a cost reduction initiative. It also takes workforce continuity.

The endless cycle of hiring and downsizing should be an embarrassment to senior leadership, especially in light of the tools available to prevent it. Unfortunately, many senior managers opt to blame the economy instead of examining their contribution to the problem.

It's difficult to sustain cost-savings when you don't involve your employees, when management changes frequently, when senior managers become enamored with the latest, greatest idea and the cycle of hiring and downsizing repeats itself endlessly.

So far we've discussed three things that leaders overlook when they're trying to reduce costs, their organization's desire to reduce costs, long-term perspective and factors influencing the sustainability of cost-savings.

Another thing that's often overlooked is the customer's continuously changing desires.

Customer Desires

Customer tastes change quickly and often. Your sales force should be asking your customers about the new challenges they face and the dreams they have. How often should this be done? Once a quarter is reasonable; more often if your offerings are short-lived.

How does this help you keep your production costs down? The insights your salespeople gain will help you keep your production aligned with your customer wishes. You can add what they want and increase your prices and profit margins accordingly. You'll also be able to eliminate what they no longer value and reduce your costs in the process. This continuous realignment with your customers' desires not only reduces production costs, it endears you to the customer, making it difficult for your competitors to get in the door.

There are a lot of advantages to monitoring your customers' desires. You've just seen two of them.

Identify those aspects of your offerings that your customers don't value and eliminate them. The savings can be huge.

As you can see, there are a number of factors outside the production process itself that can dramatically influence your ability to reduce production costs. I'll list them here again for your convenience.

- A desire to reduce costs
- A long-term perspective
- Sustainability of process improvements
- Continuous monitoring of customer desires

Let's review the core concept for production.

Core Concept – Production

> **The goal of every successful production effort is to provide the quality the customer wants, when he wants it, while continuously lowering production costs.**

Executive Summary – Production

- The customer will only pay for what he values. Avoid adding bells and whistles that aren't valued by your customer; they add cost that can't be recouped in the price

- Expedited orders and overnight deliveries are expensive Band-aids for an ailing production system

- Some of the more successful cost reduction approaches are:

  1. Benchmarking
  2. Reengineering
  3. Activity-Based Management
  4. Six Sigma
  5. Lean Manufacturing
  6. Theory of Constraints

- There are four factors outside the production process that influence your ability to successfully implement the above approaches. They are:

  1. A desire to reduce costs
  2. A long-term perspective
  3. Sustainability of process improvements
  4. Continuous monitoring of customer desires

In the first six chapters we've explored a lot of myths and misconceptions about business. In Chapter 7, *Organizational Structure*, we're going to tackle one of the more confounding aspects of business, how to structure your organization.

ORGANIZATIONAL STRUCTURE:

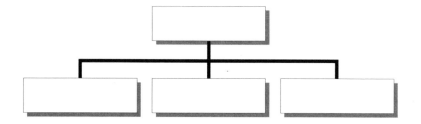

Bureaucracy -

the bane of customer satisfaction

7

Organizational Structure

What is the purpose of a successful organizational structure?

To make your customers' experience so delightful that they wouldn't think of going anywhere else.

Core Concept – Customer delight

You don't need to be an expert in organizational design to know when a company's structure is dysfunctional. Your experience is all the evidence you need. Here are two of my recent experiences. I'll let you judge which of the companies is structured with the customer in mind.

Software experience
It was time to renew my anti-virus software. I decided to upgrade my system to include internet security. I chose to download the software rather than wait for the CD. DSL isn't available in my area so I'm using a dial-up modem.

Based on my experience with other software downloads, I expected the download to take three to four hours. It took eight hours! There was no indication of download times on any of the screens I navigated. I would have chosen the CD if I had known the download was going to take 8 hours.

The second stumbling block surfaced when the software didn't automatically install or even give me a choice of whether I wanted to install now or later. The download just placed a new icon on my desktop. I spent time searching for an icon that would allow me to install the new software.

When I found the icon, I launched the install program. I watched as the software deleted the previous version as expected. Then I watched as the files for the new software were being loaded. Suddenly, the little hash marks on the indicator bar reversed direction and a message appeared that said the new files were being removed. When the indicator bar was blank again, the install program stopped and sent a message indicating that one of the required files was missing. My system was vulnerable. It had no anti-virus protection. I couldn't access my email without assuming significant risks to my data.

I went to the company's web address for contact information for the support people. I learned that if I wanted to talk to a person it would cost me 75% of the software price. As I dialed the support number, I vowed to fight that charge.

I got a recording saying that, "due to the volume of calls they couldn't take my call right now". The message asked *me* to call back later. I got the same message four times during the course of the day.

Finally, I called the customer service department and explained my dilemma. I was told that my best alternative was to go to the local software store and buy the software off the shelf. I asked why they couldn't overnight a copy of the software to me. I was told that I'd have to pay the delivery charges. I was assured that I would get a credit *as soon as I signed an affidavit* stating that I had removed the downloaded software.

Based on my experience, what do you think this organization is trying to achieve? Is it trying to satisfy its customers or is it striving for expediency and low cost? Let's compare this experience with one I had with my insurance company.

Insurance claim experience
A hailstorm damaged the roof of our house and our truck. My call to the insurance company was answered quickly. The claim representative explained that she'd have to ask some questions to gather the information she needed. She said it would take about 10 minutes; then she asked if I had time to answer the questions now. I did.

The claim representative was friendly throughout the process. It was obvious from our conversation that she was concerned about wasting my time; she even apologized for the slow response time she was experiencing with her computer. She provided the phone numbers of the adjusters who were going to handle the claims and a customer service number to call in case we hadn't heard from the adjusters in 24 hours.

One adjuster called within 2 hours, the other within 6. The adjuster for the roof explained that, due to heavy rains he might not be able to get to our roof for 2 or 3 days, but he gave us a target date. He arrived on the target date, did the inspection and granted our claim. The check arrived within a week of the adjuster's visit.

The adjuster for the car provided the names of three auto body repair shops in our area so that we could get an initial estimate quickly and conveniently. One phone call got us an appointment and an estimate the following day.

If you were the one having these two experiences, which company would you continue to use? Which one earned your loyalty? Which organization is structured well?

If the answer to the last question isn't obvious to you, don't feel like you're alone. Many business leaders don't see the connection between customer service and organizational structure. Why is this connection so elusive? Let's explore the traditional organizational structure.

The Silo Effect

As organizations grow they evolve into departments, each with a different specialty. The departments we see most often are:

- Marketing
- Sales
- Customer service
- Research and development
- Purchasing
- Production
- Human resources

- Finance
- Administration

The people in each of these departments typically view the business from the perspective of their specialty, rather than taking a more holistic view of the business. Why? Except for the upper echelon in their department, they don't get to see "the big picture." Their leaders fail to share that vision with them.

Without the big picture perspective, mid- and lower-level managers have only their departmental responsibilities to guide them in establishing performance measures for their employees. Often these performance goals conflict with goals established in other departments. This process of setting goals without regard for the impact it has on other departments is called the silo effect. Each department is operating independently of the others, as if each was in a separate silo.

You can see the silo effect at work in the software experience I described above. You can imagine the finance department determining that it's costing too much to provide telephone service to customers. The finance department puts pressure on customer service to reduce those costs. Customer service decides to post solutions to the most common problems on their website and charge for personal calls.

Neither the finance people nor the customer service group consult with production to see what's needed to reduce the number of calls resulting from download problems. By ignoring the real problem, the software company inflicts considerable pain on its customers and invites them to investigate competitors' offerings.

Some of you may be thinking, "If every company in the industry is charging for support calls, it's not a problem." Wrong! That's the mentality that the automotive industry had in the 1970s when Japanese automakers came in and took a lion's share of the United States market from the Big Three. In essence, Ford, General Motors and Chrysler invited the Japanese into their market by ignoring customers' wishes.

In an attempt to avoid the ills created by the silo effect, many companies have turned to cross-functional or multi-discipline teams. Each team is comprised of representatives from all departments. By considering all perspectives in the decision-making process, these companies are more likely to establish goals that fit their overall strategy while minimizing the possibility of conflicting goals.

Theoretically, this approach provides more balanced solutions to whatever situation the company is facing. While cross-functional teams have produced excellent results in some companies, they've failed miserably in others. Why?

- A team mentality doesn't exist in the organization.
- Senior management has a favorite child; i.e., it favors one department over the others.
- Team members don't know how to influence change when they lack "control."
- Team members vie for recognition rather than results.
- A zero sum game mentality exists; one department must lose for another to win.
- Senior management doesn't share the big picture.

Many of these obstacles can be overcome with coaching or meeting facilitation. If you're fortunate enough to have employees who possess coaching or facilitation skills, you may be able to build effective cross-functional teams yourself. Many companies turn to consultants, coaches and facilitators when their organization doesn't possess those skills or the friction between departments is too great for an insider to overcome.

If you're wondering whether developing cross-functional teams is worth the effort, ask yourself the following questions. Has your

- Sales force promised an early delivery date to gain a new customer when your production people are already facing a two month backlog?
- Finance group decided to slow payments to your vendors just as your purchasing people are trying to negotiate lower prices?
- Research and development group begun work to improve an offering when the market has been shrinking for a year or more?
- Purchasing department negotiated a long-term contract on a component for a product group you intend to discontinue?
- Product development group begun adding new features to your offering at a time when your customers are demanding lower prices?
- Collection department become more aggressive while your sales force is busy explaining broken promises to your customers?

- Marketing material touted the quality of your offerings as customer returns hit an all-time high?
- Sales force negotiated favorable payment terms with a potentially large, new customer when your company is experiencing cash flow problems?

These are a few examples of the conflicting policies you'll find in companies that fall victim to the silo effect.

Cross-functional teams can assuage the silo effect by assuring that the impact on each department is considered BEFORE the decision is made.

While cross-functional teams offer a way to avoid the silo effect, is problem avoidance all that you should expect from your organization's structure? It may be an improvement over what your company is experiencing now, but I doubt that any of you believe that problem avoidance is a solid foundation on which you can build a successful company. What's your alternative? Structure your organization around the product/service life cycle.

Product/Service Life Cycle

With this approach you're going to marry your product's life cycle to your employees' interests using cross-functional teams. This works particularly well in larger organizations where the pool of employees is large enough to possess the skills required by all stages of the product/service life cycle. Here's how it works.

Products move through a very predictable life cycle:

- Product development/introduction
- Sales growth

- Product maturity
- Market decline/disappearance

As we'll see in following sections, each stage in the product/ service life cycle

1. Places different demands on your employees.
2. Requires your employees to possess skills to meet those demands.

You can dramatically increase your employees' effectiveness by aligning their talents and interests to life cycle demands. Let's explore each stage of the life cycle to find out how you can make this work in your company.

Product development/introduction stage
This stage is fraught with tight deadlines, heavy investment, little return and all the headaches associated with trying to make a new product/service profitable. Who would want these headaches? More people than you might imagine.

In every department there are people who love working with a blank slate. Their passion for creating something new is exceeded only by the joy they get from regaling others with stories of the tremendous obstacles they've overcome.

Search all of your departments, R&D, marketing, sales, customer service, production, human resource, finance and administration, to find these people. Assemble them as a product development/introduction team, then watch in awe as they delight you with their creativity and resourcefulness.

As soon as the product is introduced these folks lose interest. It's time to pass the baton to the growth specialists.

Sales growth

This stage involves heavy promotion, dramatic sales growth as well as the production, distribution, staffing and financing challenges that accompany such growth. The product gains momentum as evidenced by increases in revenue, market share and profitability. Profits are huge because there is little competition for the new offering.

Look for people who enjoy racking up big numbers. The stories these folks love to tell are all about the numbers. You'll hear things like:

> *"When I started, we were selling 10,000 units per month. Now we're selling 1,000,000 per month."*

> *"We're adding 15 distributors a month."*

> *"We opened over 100 stores in 20 states."*

> *"Our plant doubled its production in just 15 months."*

> *"Our profits quadrupled this year."*

> *"We created 5,000 jobs in 18 months."*

These employees may not be creative with a blank slate, but they'll knock your socks off with their creativity in finding ways to generate profits quickly. They drive themselves and others hard to produce dramatic results quickly.

Growth specialists lose interest when growth slows to more modest levels, usually when competitors enter the market. It's time to pass the baton again. This time it passes from growth specialists to optimization specialists.

Product maturity
Maturity is the third stage of the product's life cycle. Your competitors have entered the market to share in the obscene profits your company enjoyed during the growth stage. Your company's focus shifts to optimizing profits during a period of "normal" revenue growth.

In the maturity stage, profit growth is more likely to come from cost reductions than revenue increases. For this stage you want to assemble a team of people who hate waste. The team should include people from all departments just as in the other phases of the product/service life cycle.

Optimization specialists' creativity lies in their ability to drive inefficiency and cost from all operating systems, marketing, sales, customer service, production, human resources and finance. No stone is left unturned in finding ways to reduce operating costs while increasing customer satisfaction. That's how they maintain solid profits in the face of competition.

The baton passes a final time when the market's interest in your offering wanes. A different set of skills is needed for the final stage of the product/service life cycle.

Market decline/disappearance
In this stage supply exceeds demand. Your company and its competitors are vying for a shrinking market. As the market declines, prices fall, making it difficult to cover costs.

If your optimization specialists did a good job in the product maturity stage, your company may be in a position to drive competitors out of the market and reestablish reasonable margins for the market. How do you accomplish that?

You establish a team of minimalists, people who get a rush from accomplishing a lot with few resources. They'll drive costs down even further; then they'll use aggressive, short-term pricing to force your competitors' prices lower.

The goal is to get the prices so low that your competitors can't be profitable at those prices. When that happens, competitors exit the market or go out of business completely. At that point, assuming a market still exists for your offering, you can raise prices and return to a reasonable profit margin.

If you and your competitors are equally strong financially, you won't be able to drive them from the market. You'll buy them or they'll buy you out of that market. For situations like this, you need a team of merger/acquisition specialists. The key here is determining whether the market is declining or disappearing. A market that's saturated and has limited future growth potential is declining. The market for an existing offering is disappearing when that offering is being replaced by something new.

Your merger/acquisition specialists can help you determine whether the market is merely declining or disappearing. They can also help you determine at what price and in which circumstances the merger/acquisition of a competitor makes sense. If neither makes sense, fold the tent and move onto markets/offerings with greater profit potential. Let your competitors lose money fighting over the dwindling market.

As you can see, the four stages of the product/service life cycle require very different skills. Match your employees' temperament and skills with the product/service life cycle stage that suits them. Then watch in amazement as your organization excels in all four stages.

Just a reminder, each stage has its own cross-functional team. You'll need someone from every department for each stage *if* you want to enjoy success in every stage.

Marrying product life cycle stages with employees' talents and interests through cross-functional teams can dramatically increase your company's success.

You may be wondering how to implement the product life cycle approach in a company that offers thousands of products. This task becomes much simpler when you realize that most products of a similar nature are combined to form strategic business units. The life of a strategic business unit parallels that of its products. As you look at each business unit, ask the following questions.

- Which of our products are the top 3 or 4 best sellers based on dollar volume?
- What has happened to the profit margins for each of these products in the last year?
- Has the unit's market share increased, held steady or declined during the year?
- Are revenues increasing, holding steady or declining?
- What's the revenue outlook for next year?
- What do we expect profit margins to be next year?
- Which competitors' products are offering the greatest competition? Why?
- How do the top sales people view your offerings vs. those of your competitors?
- What new products does this unit have in the pipeline?
- When will these new products hit the market?

- How close is competition to offering similar products?
- How well do the answers from top management agree with those of the top sales people?
- Is this unit's top management in denial about its position vs. competitors?

The answers to these questions will help you identify each business unit's life cycle stage. They'll also make it easier for you to align employees' talents and interests with the proper business unit.

A strategic business unit's life cycle mirrors the life cycle of its top three or four best selling products.

We've seen that allowing an organization to develop along functional disciplines (marketing, sales, production, human resources and finance) creates a silo effect. The silo effect produces conflicting policies that inflict pain on customers.

Companies can minimize the silo effect by using cross-functional teams. These teams avoid conflicting policies by considering the impact policies will have on each department *before* they are established. Preventing conflicting policies helps customers avoid painful experiences.

Your customers' experiences can be further enhanced by structuring your organization along product life cycle stages. Aligning your employees' interests with your products' life cycles allows them to employ their talents, skills and passion in areas where they're most likely to be successful.

Employees who enjoy their work *and* experience success daily are happier than employees whose talents and interests

are mismatched with their job requirements. As you'll see in
Chapter 8, *Work Environment*, your employees' happiness is
a vital element in creating pleasant customer experiences.
The more pleasant your customers' experiences, the more
likely they are to return.

As we've seen in Chapter 2, *Marketing,* and Chapter 3,
Selling, repeat business is more profitable than new business.
Customers who return because of a good experience don't
need the constant reminder that marketing provides. They
also don't require as much sales assistance in making their
buying decision. In essence, an organizational structure that
creates a pleasant experience for your customers will allow
you to reduce both your marketing and selling costs. These
are only two of the benefits. We'll discuss more in Chapter
8, *Work Environment*.

Life would be wonderful if we could set the organization's
structure once and leave it alone. The reality is that business
is dynamic. Products/services move through their life cycles
to be replaced by new products and services in response to
ever-changing customer needs/desires.

How can you assure that your organization is always poised
to delight your customers? The key is to keep the following
question in front of *all* of your leaders, front-line to top floor.

The Central Question
"Will adding this position or changing this policy improve
our customers' experience?" That's the question your leaders
need to ask *every day*. What happens if they don't? Your
customers "enjoy" an experience like the one described in the
software example above. That's rarely the intent, but it is

frequently the result. Why? Adding positions or changing policies without regard to the customer creates bureaucracy.

Bureaucracy is the bane of customer satisfaction. It shifts your employees' focus from your customers to other issues. Here are a few examples of how easy it is too lose sight of your customers' wishes and the consequences that ensue.

- Faulty production results in an increased number of returns from your customers. You add more quality checks into your production system. In the process you slow delivery and create backlogs. Now your customers have two reasons to leave.
- Your competitors lower prices; you feel compelled to match their prices. Your purchasing people begin searching for less expensive materials in an attempt to lower your costs. Their efforts delay ordering and, consequently, receipt of materials. The resulting material shortage slows production and delivery, once again creating backlogs.
- In an attempt to improve cash flow, finance people put pressure on the collection group to lower the age of the receivables. They forget to add the caveat, "without damaging customer relations." The result? Customers who are experiencing cash flow problems of their own are threatened rather than helped.
- Senior management's response to declining profits is a 5% across the board staff reduction. Deliveries slow, causing customers to spend more time tracking their orders. Since the customer service group has also been ravaged by cutbacks, customers find it more difficult to reach someone who can help them. Again, they have two reasons to leave.

These are just a few of the challenges managers experience at all levels in the organization. You can see how easy it is for managers to be distracted from their primary focus, your customer. It also explains why bureaucracy can be viewed as a cancer attacking your company.

Bureaucracy is like cancer in that it begins with a worthy goal and ends with the opposite result. Cancer begins with our bodies' natural defenses. These defenses are triggered when the body feels threatened. That's good; the goal of the defense system is to ensure good health. Unfortunately, our bodies' defenses sometimes perceive threats that don't exist. The result is that these defenses attack healthy parts of our bodies, cancer forms, and health declines.

Bureaucracy also begins with a worthy goal. Generally, that goal is to fix an operating problem. Unfortunately, the "fix" is usually created without considering the impact it will have on customers. The goal is good, but the result is customer dissatisfaction which translates into poor financial health. Here's how the disease progresses.

Customers who are dissatisfied don't buy as much, if they remain a customer. They're also more sensitive to price increases which means that your company will find it more difficult to raise prices even though its costs are going up. Declining sales and the inability to raise prices requires your company to gain new customers. As a result, marketing and sales expenses go up. That's on top of the higher costs your company is incurring as a result of having added people or steps to the processes being "fixed."

That's not a pretty picture, is it? How do you avoid this pain for yourselves and your customers? Go back to the central question, "Will adding this position or changing this policy improve our customers' experience?" If the answer is "No," don't make the change. Don't let cancer eat away at your company's health.

Whenever a new position or policy change is suggested, ask, "How will this enhance our customers' experience?"

By continually asking this question, you assure that it's at the fore of every manager's and every employee's mind. That's how you avoid bureaucracy.

Now that we've placed the customer as the focal point of organizational structure, let's see whether there are any other misconceptions we need to address.

Other Misconceptions

The lack of customer focus is, without a doubt, the most frequent failing of organizational structures. The second failing I encounter is misaligned reporting relationships between managers and employees. In the past decade, the consensus has been that flatter organizations are more efficient because they remove layers of bureaucracy. Has that proven true? Has the efficacy of the manager-worker relationship been improved with a flatter organization chart?

Manager-Worker Relationships

The late Dr. Elliott Jaques of George Washington University extensively researched manager-worker relationships. The results of his research shaped his theory and formed the basis of his book, *Requisite Organization.*[19]

---

[19] Elliott Jaques, *Requisite Organization*, Cason Hall, 1997

I won't relate the entire theory to you, but there is one aspect of his research that I find particularly helpful when working with my clients. Dr. Jaques attributes much of the frustration that managers and their employees experience to differences in mental complexity. What is mental complexity?

Dr. Jaques defines mental complexity as the timeframe used by an employee in planning her work. A frontline worker typically plans her work a day at a time, occasionally looking a week ahead. Her immediate supervisor looks a week to a month ahead. The mid-level plans six months to a year down the road, while the CEO's planning horizon is three to five years into the future.

The key to avoiding frustrations associated with differences in mental complexity is to create an organizational structure that aligns employees and supervisors according to their mental complexity. In other words, don't have a frontline worker (daily planning) reporting to a mid-level supervisor (planning six months to a year out); both become frustrated.

Let's examine the source of the frustration in the situation just described. The front-line employee brings a question or problem to a mid-level manager. The manager resents being drawn into things that no longer interest her so she either

1. Dismisses the question leaving the employee to her own devices, or
2. Delays dealing with the situation, preventing the employee from completing the task.

With either response, the manager sends the message that the employee's needs are insignificant, which leads the employee to feel that her work isn't valued. Resentment builds; a clash of "personalities" is inevitable.

There are several ways to avoid these frustrations:

1. Consider the mental complexity of the job *before* starting the hiring process; then hire accordingly
2. Reassign work when the mental complexity of a job varies widely from task to task
3. Revamp your organizational structure so that you don't have an employee reporting to a manager whose mental complexity is two or more levels higher than the employee's
4. Managers should have employees report to a qualified fellow employee for work the manager finds tedious

Designing a job and creating a reporting relationship which avoids these frustrations is not difficult. It does require some time and effort; unfortunately, more than most managers are willing to invest. Make the investment! You'll not only delight your customers, you'll avoid frustrating yourself and your employees.

Align the mental complexity of the job, the employee's natural planning timeframe and the manager's planning cycle and you'll increase your organization's ability to delight your customers.

Let's take a moment to review what we've discussed.

Core Concept – Organizational Structure

The purpose of organizational structure is to make your customers' experience so delightful that they wouldn't think of going anywhere else.

Executive Summary – Organizational Structure

- Bureaucracy is the bane of customer satisfaction.

- Staff additions and policy decisions designed to "fix" operating problems usually create bureaucracy.

- The way to avoid bureaucracy is to ask, "How will this new employee or new policy enhance our customers' experience?"

- As organizations grow, employees tend to view the business from the perspective of their specialty rather than a holistic view of the company. This is called the silo effect.

- The silo effect fosters a lack of coordination among departments resulting in disjointed and, often, conflicting decisions. The customer becomes a victim.

- The silo effect can be minimized through cross-functional, multi-discipline teams.

- Another way to avoid the silo effect and improve your customers' experiences is to structure your organization to match the various stages of the product life cycle.

- Dr. Elliott Jaques states that organizational structures are more effective when employees' planning timeframes are matched with the planning requirements of the job and their manager's planning cycle.

With a firm grip on the handle of organizational structure, let's turn our attention to the work environment. Does the work environment influence more than your company's ability to attract high-caliber talent? Join me in Chapter 8 and, together, we'll find out.

WORK ENVIRONMENT:

How do your employees view their work?

8

Work Environment

What do you want your work environment to do for you?

To make you the employer of choice in your area while assuring your customers a pleasant experience every time they deal with your employees.

Core Concept – Employee delight

My friend, John, worked for a regional CPA firm. Within weeks of being hired he was assigned to audit a small manufacturing company. His firm's procedures required that he underline the heading of each audit schedule.

John completed the audit in 2/3 the time it had taken in previous years. It's important to note that audit work is typically billed on a fixed fee basis. Completing the job early meant that he could earn more revenue for the firm with the time he'd saved.

Upon completing his review of John's work, the managing partner called John into his office, informed him that he had forgotten to underline the headings of *two* schedules and asked him to be more careful in the future.

John was appalled! He was expecting to be congratulated for making the job more profitable or complimented on the quality of his work (there weren't any errors); instead, the managing partner commented on a trivial oversight. My friend immediately started looking for another job.

My purpose in relating this experience is to demonstrate how easy it is to lose an employee who has the desire and ability to improve your bottom line. Yet, John's leaving is not the worst thing this firm could've experienced. Let's see what kind of employee he could have become had he stayed.

Dissatisfied Employee
Let's assume that John hadn't changed jobs. Would the prospect of going to work put a smile on his face? Would he be sporting a "conquer the world" attitude? Not likely! Instead, lethargy would have supplanted enthusiasm. Every task would have become such a burden that John would have been doing just enough to keep from getting fired.

If that were the only consequence of his unhappiness you might be able to live with it, but you and I both know that there's more to this problem than an underperforming employee. There's the impact his attitude has on others, employees and customers alike. Let's examine the behavior he's likely to exhibit.

Unpleasant

John wouldn't be pleasant to be around. He wouldn't be spiteful (that's not his nature), but it would be obvious to everyone around him that he's simply going through the motions.

John's likely to develop a "glass half-empty" mindset. The negativity he exhibits will weigh heavily on his fellow employees. It may even cause them to embrace that outlook. When that happens he becomes a cancer eating away the productivity of the entire department. Wait! There's more!

Do you think his attitude will be any different in his dealings with the customer? John's likely to view everything being asked of him as a chore. Anything that disrupts his schedule becomes a nuisance. Is that what you want customers to feel, that they're an inconvenience? You're a consumer; you've dealt with people who treated you as a nuisance. You also know how you respond to that type of treatment.

In addition to being generally disagreeable, lowering employee morale and driving off your customers, here's what else you can expect from John. He won't be improving his skills because they aren't going to be appreciated anyway. As a manager, that means the capability of your department diminishes over time as does your ability to serve your customers. He's not finished yet!

John is not going to help you recruit top-notch people because he knows they won't be appreciated. In fact, John's negativity and minimalist work ethic have probably driven off some of your better workers. What you have left is an ensemble of unhappy, unmotivated and incompetent employees. Now your customers have the privilege of dealing with a whole series of employees with John's attitude. Isn't that wonderful?

As a consumer, you've been in companies where every employee exhibits the attitudes I just described. The question is, "How long did you remain a customer?" Most of us won't do business with companies whose employees treat us as inconveniences. Why should we?

Dissatisfied employees under-perform in their work, lower employee morale, fail to improve their skills, refuse to recruit top-notch people and drive away your customers. Compelling arguments for a good work environment, wouldn't you agree?

Now that you have a sense for how vital a good work environment is, let's see what it takes to create one.

Creating the Environment

Your employees can't help your customers feel good unless they feel good. The question then is, "How can you assure that your employees have a reason to feel good *every day*?"

There are six factors that influence your employees' satisfaction with themselves and their employment:

1. Being valued by the employer
2. Being respected and supported by peers
3. Experiencing success

4. Being recognized for success – emotionally and
    financially
5. Experiencing growth - personally and financially
6. Teaching others to become more successful

Let's look at each of these in more detail.

Being valued
Imagine coming to work knowing that your:

- Colleagues solicit your advice
- Boss involves you in decisions affecting your work
- Ideas get a fair hearing and, if they fit the company's
  vision, are implemented quickly

Many of you are thinking, "If I had a job like that, I'd feel
like I was in employment heaven." Of course you would!
The need to be valued is universal. Abraham Maslow[20]
identified this as ego or esteem need, a need for a "high level
of self-respect and respect from others in order to feel
satisfied, self-confident and valuable." Let's draw upon your
experience to see how accurate Maslow's insight is.

I'm sure that each of you has experienced days when your
ideas are enthusiastically embraced and days when you've
felt that you might as well have been talking to the wall. Do
you remember the emotions you experienced?

On the good days, were you pumped? Did you feel like you
had even more to give? Were you anxious to make an even

---

[20] Creator of Maslow's Hierarchy of Needs, a theory of human motivation

greater contribution? If, at that moment, a customer had come to you wanting help, how would you have reacted?

Would you have offered your biggest smile, demonstrated your genuine interest in their welfare and extended your best effort to resolve their dilemma?

What about the bad days? The days when no one will listen to you; the days you feel that you're being taken for granted? How would you react to a customer needing help? To some degree, it depends on the frequency with which you experience bad days, doesn't it?

If a bad day is a rarity, you may have enough emotional reserves to provide quality service to the customer. Will that be true if you've experienced months or years of bad days? Will there be any emotional reserves left? If not, what's the customer likely to experience? Your emotional distress?

I'm confident that your answers to these questions affirm the need for a work environment in which employees are valued.

If you want your customers to feel valued, value your employees.

It isn't enough that you value your employees; your employees must value and respect one another. That brings us to the second factor influencing employee satisfaction, peer respect and support. Here are tips for accomplishing that goal.

Peer respect and support
If you value your employees, but they don't value each other you've lost the war. I can't begin to count the number of

times that I've seen business leaders tolerate disrespectful treatment of one employee by another. Why do they tolerate this behavior? Here are a couple of explanations.

Untouchables

Bad behavior is tolerated because the disrespectful employee is a "top performer," family member or co-owner. I placed "top performer" in quotation marks because my experience has been that the costs these people create in terms of employee turnover, lost productivity and disruptive behavior are much greater than the value they create.

In each of these situations it is imperative that you educate the disrespectful employee on the inappropriateness of his behavior. If the person refuses to change, you have two options, let him go or isolate him. It may not be possible to terminate a family member or remove a co-owner, but you may be able to limit his interaction with employees who aren't strong enough to defend themselves against his abusive behavior. Isolation is an alternative to termination.

Confrontation

Some managers tolerate disrespectful behavior because they hate confrontation and will do almost anything to avoid confronting the offending employee.

If you happen to be one of these managers, find a coach who can help you develop a way of comfortably dealing with these situations. There are techniques for getting a problem employee to become introspective so he can see the havoc he's creating. The goal is to help the offending employee to see how he's creating problems for himself; it's not intended to admonish him for his behavior.

If you've ever tried to avoid disciplining an offending employee by assigning the task to a subordinate, you know it doesn't work. The offending employee always appeals his case to you which puts you back where you started.

If you want your employees to respect one another, you must set the example by showing them respect and intervening when you see them being disrespectful to one another. Mutual respect among employees is vital, but to get to superior customer service, your employees must go beyond respect and support one another.

Support
Support means that you and your employees help one another by providing what is needed when it's needed. The need could be information, resources, assistance, encouragement or plaudits.

Employees who feel valued and respected by their boss and peers demonstrate a strong desire to help others. Yet, there are times when desire isn't enough. The employee simply doesn't have the experience, knowledge or resources to help. At times like these he must look to others in the organization for help. The keys for creating a supportive environment are:

- The employee's awareness that he doesn't have to have all the answers
- Confidence in his fellow employees' willingness to stop what they're doing to help him when he needs it
- Knowledge of the limits of his authority
- An awareness of the skills and knowledge each of his colleagues possess

Customers can tell in an instant whether or not they are going to have a good experience. When the customer walks into a business where people are enthusiastic about their work, there is electricity in the air, an excitement that is contagious. That's how the customer *knows* that he's going to have a pleasant experience.

When the customer visits a business where the employees are simply going through the motions, he knows that getting anyone to acknowledge him, much less help him, is going to be a chore. Which experience do you want your customers to have?

> *Create a respectful, supportive environment for your employees and they'll create one for your customers.*

When the first two factors of employee satisfaction are in place, the employee feels valued and he's being respected and supported by his peers, it's time to make sure that he's experiencing success.   Amazingly, that's the topic of the next section.

Experiencing success
I'd like you to think of two people. The first is someone you consider successful. Got a clear picture? Good! Now think of someone who seems to accept whatever life gives them. Which of these two people is more generous with their time and energy? If you're not sure, let's explore a few more questions together.

Would you agree that successful people usually feel that life is better than they thought possible? Is it also fair to say that those who accept what life hands them often feel that life's promise remains just out of reach? Is it easier to give from the realm of riches or province of poverty?

Successful people are typically generous because their lives are filled with a sense of abundance. Those who lack this sense are inclined to hoard. They fear that what they give away will never be replaced, that their generosity will leave them further impoverished.

What does this mean in terms of employee morale and customer delight? The more your employees experience success, the richer their lives become, emotionally and financially. The richer their lives, the more willing they are to share their abundance with your customers. The question is, "How do you help your employees gain this sense of abundance?"

Goals
Is it fair to say that it's difficult to feel successful, to gain a sense of accomplishment, without a goal? Is it also fair to say that many of your fellow employees don't set goals for themselves? Why is that? The answer I get most often is, "fear of failure."

Many people avoid setting goals for themselves because they fear failure. Interestingly, it is the fear of failure that drives us to achieve a goal once it's set. Help your employees enjoy greater success; help them overcome the natural tendency to avoid setting goals for themselves.

Before we discuss how to do this, allow me to offer a caveat. Some of your employees will say that they have goals. In reality, they have fantasies. What's the difference?

People with goals have a game plan. They know at least the first few steps they need to take to achieve their goals and they're willing to take those steps.

People with fantasies dream of what might be without developing a plan for making it a reality. If an employee claims to have a goal, ask him what steps he's going to take to achieve his goal. If he has a plausible answer, he has a goal. If not, he's fantasizing.

Once you've opened your employee's heart to goal setting here are a few things to help him achieve his goals.

1. Assure that the employee's goals are reasonable, that he has a better than 50% chance of success. Yes, his goals should be stretch goals, but they should be reasonable in light of his experience, capabilities and self-confidence. Don't allow the employee to set himself up for failure.

2. Provide feedback mechanisms that allow the employee to monitor his progress. Without feedback, your employee is likely to overlook the progress he's making and become discouraged. Most goals take longer to achieve than originally envisioned.

3. Believe in your employee's ability to achieve his goal. The stronger your belief in his ability to succeed the more likely he is to prove you right.

4. Provide assistance only when asked; otherwise, you diminish the employee's sense of accomplishment. At times, in situations where the cost of failure is small, you may need to let the employee fail in order for him to learn what behaviors prevented his success.

The establishment and achievement of goals are vital to your employees' ability to experience success. Their success is the key to the sense of abundance they need to share their "wealth" with your customers.

Achieving a goal is its own reward. Employees who experience success gain a sense of satisfaction, personal growth and increased confidence. Not a bad payoff, but you can enhance their returns by assuring public recognition of their accomplishments. That's the fourth factor influencing employee satisfaction.

Recognition
Public recognition is another way of satisfying the ego/esteem need described by Maslow. Ego is a powerful motivator. Each of us possesses it by virtue of our humanity. It's that part of us that wants others to know that we're making significant contributions to the company's success.

Leaders who understand ego needs realize that recognition serves as both reward and incentive in satisfying this need. Recognition serves as a reward because it satisfies your employees' esteem needs, the need to feel valued. It also serves as an incentive because employees desire to relive the satisfaction gained from their achievements, personal growth, enhanced confidence and public recognition.

Recognition programs are as varied as the companies employing them. The more successful programs consider the company's style. Southwest Airlines hosts delightfully zany, "employee appreciation" parties which makes sense since they hire fun-loving people. A company whose employees view themselves as premier service providers may use diamond pins. Each diamond in the pin represents another level of service success. Companies with low-paying jobs find "on-the-spot" monetary rewards are a great way to reward people with limited incomes. Whatever plan you design, make sure that:

- Everyone has fun
- The reward is deserved
- The praise is genuine
- Employees are rewarded frequently

Recognition allows your employees to feel valued which makes it easier for them to value your customers.

Success and its recognition are vital to employees' esteem needs, but how often do your employees need to experience success to enjoy their work environment. That brings us to the fifth factor influencing employee satisfaction, experiencing growth.

Experiencing growth
Unfortunately, the satisfaction of success is fleeting. Don't take my word for it. Think of a goal you achieved. Recall the joy you felt. How long did that feeling last?

For many of us, the satisfaction of success has a life span of a few days. After that life returns to "normal" and we become mired in the drudgery of day-to-day work. The excitement we experienced only a few days earlier seems a distant memory. We long for that excitement again.

Your employees experience the same emotions. Help them avoid this roller coaster ride. Provide new challenges, new goals and new opportunities for them. Make it possible for

your employees to enjoy success frequently. The shorter the
interval between each success the more enjoyable the job
becomes. How do you help your employees experience
success frequently? Raise the bar.

Raise the bar
Don't allow your employees to become complacent; after
each success raise the bar for them. Many employees fear
that the more they accomplish the more that you'll expect of
them. That's a natural reaction, but it's short-sighted. What
they don't realize is that without new challenges their jobs:

- Become boring; without new challenges every day is
  the same as the day before
- Are devoid of opportunities for the satisfaction and
  public recognition that success brings
- Limit their value to the company which limits their
  financial future

It's your job to raise the bar, to find ways of challenging your
employees so that they can experience growth. Their skills
and abilities need to grow for your company to serve your
customers' ever-changing needs. Their job satisfaction needs
to grow for them to continue to delight your customers.
Their confidence needs to grow so that they can accept even
greater challenges in the future.

I may need to clarify a point here. I'm not suggesting that
raising the bar should involve more hours spent in the
workplace. My experience is that approximately 20% of
what most employees do has little, if any, value. Eliminate
this waste and your employees will have plenty of time to
successfully accomplish what you ask of them as you raise
the bar on their performance.

If you share the rationale for raising the bar described above and you demonstrate your interest in making your employees' work more exciting and financially rewarding, they'll reward you with superior performance.

Employees need to grow to be happy with their work environment. When they're happy, they're more likely to pass that joy along to your customers.

At some point, your employees may become so adept at their jobs that you'll find it difficult to challenge them frequently enough to keep them happy. That's when it's time to make them teachers. It's another way of publicly recognizing their success and keeping them challenged.

Teaching
Last week, one of my most successful clients told me, "Dale, I have everything I need. I want to help others enjoy the success I have." Teaching is an important element of job satisfaction and another form of recognition for your most successful employees.

These employees no longer have anything to prove to themselves. Indeed, their job satisfaction often wanes because they've become adept at handling new challenges.

The way to bring excitement back into their work is to help them move beyond their personal needs to the greater community need. Let them experience the joy that comes from helping others enjoy the success they've already achieved. Give them an opportunity to shine in front of their peers. Help them gain the recognition they so richly deserve.

As your employees become more successful they'll want to share their success with others. Give them the opportunity. Have them lead discussion groups, facilitate workshops, lead new employee orientations, provide demonstrations. The format isn't important. It's the opportunity to share their wisdom with their colleagues that allows your employees to increase their job satisfaction and gain greater recognition.

Your employees aren't the only beneficiaries. When employees get into the teaching mode they begin educating your customers as well. As your customers learn what options are available to them and the advantages and disadvantages of each, they become more comfortable with their decisions. The more comfortable they are in their dealing with your company, the less likely they are to visit your competitors.

Teaching is the ultimate form of public recognition. Help your employees teach others how to be successful and you'll enjoy both an energetic workforce and loyal customers.

As you can see, a good work environment is a key ingredient for creating both a successful workforce and great customer service. For more insights into how to create a work environment that produces great employees and superior customer service, check out these books:

Raving Fans: A Revolutionary Approach to Customer Service[21] by Kenneth H. Blanchard

---

[21] Kenneth Blanchard, *Raving Fans: A Revolutionary Approach to Customer Service,* William Morrow & Co. 1993

This excellent book is replete with examples of
incredible customer service and descriptions of the
environments that fostered them.

Making the EXCEPTIONAL Normal[22]
by Dale Furtwengler

This book provides a systematic approach for creating
an environment that encourages your employees to
ever-increasing levels of success while helping them
enjoy all of the benefits described above.

Some of you may be thinking that you're not high enough in
the organization to create this kind of work environment or
that your group doesn't deal with customers. Let's explore
these beliefs.

1. You can create an environment like the one just
    described *for your group.* You may not be able to
    effect this change in the whole organization, but you
    can in your group.

    The results your group gets will get the attention of
    others. When they ask how you do it, share your
    approach with them. Then sit back and watch as your
    approach gradually gets adopted by other departments
    in your company.

    One person can make a difference *from anywhere in
    the organization.* Why not you?

---

[22] Dale Furtwengler, *Making the EXCEPTIONAL Normal*, Peregrine
Press 1997

2. Even though your group doesn't deal directly with the public, your policies and procedures can influence the customer's experience. Administrative rules that result in delayed deliveries, reduced or slowed service, or greater burdens on the customer diminish customer satisfaction.

    Unhappy employees are likely to create rules that share their pain with customers. Conversely, happy employees look for ways to make the customer experience pleasant.

If you want to create a work environment that delights customers, make sure that your employees:

- Feel valued
- Are respected and supported by peers
- Experience success
- Are recognized for success - emotionally and financially
- Experience growth - personally and financially
- Teach others to be successful

Remember, superior customer service offers huge paybacks. Here are three biggies:

1. Repeat business
2. Customer referrals
3. Higher than usual prices

As I'm sure many of you have experienced, the work environment I just described is a rarity. That's a sad reality. The reasons for this lie in the misconceptions that managers have about staffing, compensation and leadership. What are these misconceptions? Let's find out.

Other Misconceptions

During my fourteen years of consulting with clients I've found that the biggest mistakes are made in the hiring process. One of the most common is overestimating the number of people it takes to get the job done. Let's find out why this happens.

Staffing

At the risk of being redundant, I'm going to use an example I used in Chapter 6, *Production*. Feel free to skim past it, if you recall the example.

A new opportunity presented itself to one of my clients. It was obvious that he was excited by this new prospect. While he was explaining his good fortune to me he declared, "I need five more people!" This company employed 55 people. He was looking at a 9% increase in staff.

As we explored the "need" for five new people, we found that the skills he needed already existed inside the company. "But," he said, "everyone is busy, they don't have time to take on additional work." Yes, they were all busy, but the real question was, "Busy doing what?"

Further investigation revealed that the employees whose help we needed were spending significant amounts of time on work that had little value. By shifting their time from low value work to this new opportunity, my client was able to accomplish his goal while adding only one new employee.

Now imagine this scenario, absent the analysis my client and I performed, being played out again and again in Fortune 500 size companies. Is it any wonder that we hear about layoffs of 30,000 people in one company?

Unbridled enthusiasm and the mistaken belief that employees are spending all their time on meaningful work combine to cause the endless cycle of hiring and downsizing that large corporations have experienced for the past two decades. These cycles are painful for laid off employees and their families, for managers who have to decide who goes and who stays, for survivors who experience heavier workloads and stockholders who bear the cost of these early retirement/ termination packages.

The price of this management failing is too great. Having said that, I don't believe it's fair to criticize without offering a solution, so here's an approach that I use when working with my clients.

Pre-hiring process review
Do the process review *before* adding staff. In Chapter 6, *Production*, we explored a plethora of process review techniques including Benchmarking, Reengineering, Activity-Based Cost Management, Six Sigma, Theory of Constraints and Lean Manufacturing. All of these techniques are designed to uncover system inefficiencies. Let's get ahead of the curve. Let's review processes *before* making the decision to add staff.

When the inclination to hire hits the manager, he needs to take a deep breath and think about how to accomplish his dream *without* adding staff. How? He can employ one of the

techniques listed above or he can simply ask himself the
following questions:

- What am I trying to accomplish?
- Will the achievement of my goal add value to the
  customer experience?
- What skills are needed to accomplish this goal?
- Which of those skills already exist in my workforce?
- How am I currently utilizing the employees
  possessing those skills?

These are the questions I asked my client in the example
above. That analysis took us less than ½ hour to complete. It
doesn't take much time to avoid the pain of overstaffing.

I realize that some managers are not adept at or may not
enjoy process evaluation. Others may not possess the
utilitarian nature necessary to see opportunities to avoid
overstaffing. So let's help them, shall we?

In Chapter 6, *Production*, each of the cost reduction
techniques described involved teams whose express purpose
was the review of processes. Why don't we have some of
these teams help managers evaluate their hiring plans *before*
they're implemented?

I'm sure some of you are bristling at that thought. After all,
you don't want someone else telling you how to run your
department, do you? Before you answer, let's explore your
options.

1. You can have someone help you avoid overstaffing.
2. In the future, you can tell some of your staff that you
   can no longer afford to keep them.

You can avoid the unpleasantness of option two and enhance your work environment *without* giving up control. It's simple! Draw on the talents of those with a penchant for efficiency to help you achieve your goal without adding staff. Even if you're skilled in process evaluation, it doesn't hurt to get an external perspective on what your group's doing. If additional staff is needed, the decision on whom to hire is still yours.

Not only is the solution to overstaffing simple, the upside is incredible. Here are some of the benefits you'll gain:

- A happier workforce
- Happier customers; they're dealing with employees who really enjoy their work
- Higher profits in good times; the savings generated by not adding staff goes directly to the bottom line
- Higher profits during difficult economic times; you're not paying for huge separation packages
- More productivity because your workers aren't fretting over the uncertainty of their future
- Consistent increases in productivity. A stable workforce has time to focus on process improvement. A constantly changing workforce uses its time to redesign processes to fit "survivors'" skills and time limitations

With all these benefits is there any reason to avoid the pre-hiring process review? With a solution this simple, is there any reason why so many people, employees and managers alike, should have experienced the pain and anguish of the past twenty years?

Five simple questions can help you avoid overstaffing and its inevitable consequence, downsizing.

The second misconception that we're going to discuss is the role money plays in establishing a good work environment.

Compensation
Many managers are under the mistaken belief that employees are motivated, first and foremost, by money. While that's true for some employees, it's not true for the vast majority. If you doubt that, read Fortune Magazine's articles associated with their "100 Best Companies to Work For" lists. See what the employees interviewed say about what's important to them. You'll find that they want to be valued, respected and recognized. They want the opportunity to grow personally and professionally. In essence, they want all the things we discussed above.

In case you're still not convinced, Meridian Partners, a retained executive search consulting firm, says that their studies show that "A" players cost only about 20% more than "B" players even though they produce 50% to 130% more than the "B" players.[23]

If the "A" players were truly motivated by money, they'd be demanding compensation more commensurate with the results they're producing. Meridian's study shows that the "A" players are often more interested in their long-term prospects than their immediate compensation.

---

[23] Bisk Education, Inc., Financial Accounting & Management Report, February 2002

Why am I harping on this point? I see too many managers throwing money at talented, unhappy employees in hopes of keeping them. These managers don't consider the possibility that there could be other reasons behind their employees' dissatisfaction. If there are, money won't solve the problem.

In my youth, I succumbed to an offer of more money only to find that a few months later I was still unhappy with my job. Money cannot fill the gap left by a missing component of job satisfaction. In my case, I'd become bored with the job. Both my employer and I made the mistake thinking that more money would solve the problem. It didn't. I left a few months later. All we did was postpone the inevitable.

Don't make the mistake of throwing money at the problem; it's rare that money is the real issue even though that's the one given most often by employees. When approached about a raise, ask your employee:

- What do you like about your job?
- What aspects of your job would you rather avoid?
- If you could try something new, what would it be?

The answers to these questions will give you insights into the real issues behind the employee's request for more money. It may be money. If it is, you'll learn that as well.

Now that we've discussed how not to use compensation, let's see what's involved in using compensation effectively. Here are the key considerations:

- Reward vs. incentive
- Self-monitoring systems
- Flexibility

Reward vs. incentive

Compensation may be viewed as either a reward or an incentive. It's considered a reward if the raise or bonus (cash, stock options, other benefits) is decided at the end of the salary review period.

In other words, if you don't establish goals with your employees and tie future raises or bonuses to these goals, compensation is being used as a reward.

If you establish goals with your employees, tie compensation to these goals and allow the employees' success to dictate their level of compensation, you're using compensation as an incentive. Let's talk about rewards first.

Reward

There are several dangers involved in using compensation as a reward. Here are just a few:

- The employee's view of their worth is often higher than the manager's. The result? Conflict.
- Managers using compensation as a reward typically don't establish measures to assist them in setting the amount of raise. This makes it difficult for the manager to support his evaluation of his employee's worth, a situation which assures that someone won't be happy. The manager won't be happy if he caves to the employee's demands. The employee won't be happy if the manager refuses to budge from his position. Compromises often result in neither party being happy.
- The employee learns at salary review time what was really expected of him. It's too late! He can't possibly remedy the situation now. He feels cheated.

A manager who has not communicated his expectations invites the following retort, "Why didn't you tell me sooner? I'd have been happy to do what you wanted had I known what it was. I don't think it's fair to penalize me for something I didn't know." Imagine trying to answer this retort while trying to hold onto a valued employee.

You can avoid this unpleasantness by using compensation as an incentive. What difference does it make? Let's see.

Incentive

Whether your incentive program takes the form of a raise, bonus, stock option or other benefit, it involves clear communication of expectations and compensation for the *coming* review period. This is as true for a new-hire as it is for a twenty-year veteran.

With a new hire, you're communicating your expectations for the next 90 to 120 days. He knows what his compensation will be during this time. At the end of the probationary period, you and your employee should jointly establish new expectations based on what you've both learned about the employee's skills and abilities. The two of you will agree on how much compensation the employee will receive for each expectation met, just as you did with longer-term employees.

Think about the dangers we discussed in the *Reward* section. Aren't they virtually eliminated by using compensation as an incentive? Yes, the possibility of miscommunication exists in every dialogue, but I think you'll agree that the likelihood of conflict diminishes dramatically with the use of the incentive approach.

Disagreements over compensation can be dramatically reduced by using compensation as an incentive instead of a reward.

Before we leave our discussion of incentive compensation, I'd like to share a couple of approaches that have worked well for me. One approach deals with raises, the other bonus arrangements.

Raises
If you want to use the incentive approach for raises, but you don't want to establish a separate monetary amount for each goal, try the following approach.

Create three tiers of employee performance, improving, steady and at risk. Tie the raises of each tier to a government price index. The consumer price index and producer price index are two frequently used indices. Here's how it works.

The "improving" group can expect raises of 1% to 7% *more* than the price index increase depending on the level of success they experience. Let's assume you're using the consumer price index to establish raises and the index rises 2% during the course of the year. Let's further assume that one of your improving employees accomplishes all of his goals. This employee's raise could be as high as 9%, the 2% index increase plus the maximum 7% allowed for achieving all of his goals.

The "steady" group is comprised of those who do a reliable job with little supervision, but aren't improving. These folks earn a raise equivalent to the index increase, 2% in this example.

The "at risk" group is comprised of underperformers. They don't get a raise. Instead, they'll get guidance and support designed to help them move from the "at risk" group to the "steady" group. Warning! Make sure these employees are working harder at earning their continued employment than you are. If you're trying harder than they are, cut them loose. It's never going to work.

***When using the incentive approach with raises,
use performance tiers and a government price index to
help you determine and communicate the
raises your employees can expect.***

This approach works well when you don't want to establish monetary raises for each performance goal. Now, let's see how the incentive approach works with bonuses.

Bonus arrangements
When designing incentive bonuses you'll need to wear two hats. The first hat is your manager's hat. Ask yourself:

- What am I trying to accomplish?
- What's it worth to the company?
- What's fair for the employee who achieves this goal?

When you feel you've structured a bonus that provides both a worthwhile incentive for the employee and a good return for the company, switch hats. Become the employee. Ready? Now, find ways to abuse the program. That's right; you need to learn how to beat the system.

There are two statements that I can make with absolute certainty.

1. Every system can be beaten
2. There are always a few employees, especially those motivated by money, who abuse the system.

Once you've determined how the system can be beaten and who is likely to abuse the program, you need to estimate what the abuse will cost the company. By identifying the potential cost, you determine your course of action.

If only one or two people are likely abusers and the cost is minimal, go ahead with the program. If you expect one or two abusers and the cost is high, consider whether you really want to continue employing these folks. If a significant percentage of the employees are likely to abuse the system, go back to the drawing board. You need to redesign the bonus arrangement.

When designing bonus arrangements, you need to wear two hats; the manager's hat to design the program and the employee's hat to see how you can abuse the system.

The use of the incentive approach, whether for raises or bonuses, leads to the need for self-monitoring feedbacks systems, our next topic for discussion.

Self-monitoring systems
One of the keys to any incentive program is the employee's ability to monitor his own progress. Two crucial components of effective feedback system are simplicity and visibility.

The Pizza Hut example in Chapter 6, *Production*, demonstrates a wonderful blend of simplicity and high visibility. The franchisee used a white board to track the percent of "on time deliveries, this week, without any accidents." The goal is easy to understand; the white board is displayed above the counter for high visibility to employees and customers alike.

Similarly, in their book, **Lean Thinking,**[24] Womack and Jones offer several examples of simple, highly-visible systems that provide timely, useful information. In fact, many of their clients found the feedback from these systems more useful than the information gained from their sophisticated software systems.

High visibility helps your employees maintain focus while affording both you and them the ability to monitor their progress toward the goal. When you and your employees are both using the same information to monitor progress, the likelihood of a dispute during a salary/bonus review drops almost to zero.

Simple, highly-visible, self-monitoring systems minimize salary/bonus disputes by giving your employees access to the same information you use in evaluating performance.

Once you've decided whether to use compensation as a reward or an incentive *and* you've developed self-monitoring systems to help your employees maintain focus, it's time to turn your attention to the third element of an effective compensation program, flexibility.

---

[24] James Womack & Daniel Jones, *Lean Thinking*, Simon & Schuster, 1996

Flexibility

There are only two points that I'd like to make here. First, we tend to forget that employees are individuals whose lives are dynamic. Their family situations vary widely; they face different health issues, have different financial needs and lifestyle goals. All of these needs change over time.

Second, compensation is more than salaries and bonuses. When many of us think of compensation, we think of salary. Yet, the benefit programs we offer are compensation as well. The key to an effective compensation program is combining salaries/bonuses (whatever form they might take) with the kinds of benefits that each of us needs at various times during our lives. Let's revisit those needs now.

Until we start a family, we're typically concerned only with our salary and a decent health insurance program. When we start a family, our needs change. We need life insurance to protect our loved ones and to cover the mortgage on our new home. We also gain an appreciation for disability insurance. Later, we're concerned with financing college for our kids and providing care for our aged parents. Of course, we'd like to retire someday. Oh, by the way, wouldn't it be great if we could pay for some of this stuff with pre-tax dollars?

Section 125 of the Internal Revenue Code allows companies to create "cafeteria plans." These are benefit plans that allow employees to choose from a "menu" of items designed to satisfy the needs they currently face in their lives. Cafeteria plans allow employees to pay for these needs with pre-tax dollars which means they get more bang for the buck with each wage increase.

Construct a program that allows your employees to choose the form of compensation that's most valuable to them. The ability to choose greatly enhances employees' enjoyment of their work environment.

Flexibility in a compensation program means that an employee can choose the form of compensation that is most valuable to him, given his current life situation.

For those of you who would like more information on designing compensation programs, here are a couple of books that will help.

The Compensation Handbook: A State-of-the-Art Guide to Compensation Strategy and Design Lance A. Berger and Dorothy R. Berger – Editors in Chief, McGraw Hill, Fourth Edition

Gainsharing and Productivity: A Guide to Planning, Implementation, and Development Robert J. Doyle, Jr. Anacom 1983

Now that we've completed our discussion of the three factors involved in creating a compensation program, let's turn our attention to one of the most talked about and least understood aspects of the work environment, leadership.

Leadership

Library shelves are filled with books on leadership. I'm not going to recap all the principles they discuss. I'm sure that brought a smile to your face. There's only one point I'd like to make regarding leadership; it's all about psychology. The psychology we employ determines the results we get.

No, I'm not suggesting that you need a degree in psychology. You do need self-awareness, an understanding of your motivations, how you react in different situations and with different personalities. Understanding yourself allows you to understand others more readily. We are, after all, cut from the same cloth. That's been proven time and again in the research that's been done on human behavior.

Here are a few things that psychology can teach us about human behavior, ours as well as our employees'.

- Influence is more powerful than control.
- You cannot control others without their consent.
- We create resistance for the very ideas we're trying to promote when we tell people what to do rather than engaging them in what needs to be done.
- Many people don't set goals for themselves because they fear failure.
- We often set priorities on the basis of what we like to do instead of what's most important for our success.
- The language we use influences the results we get.

This knowledge is essential for understanding the needs of those whom we lead. Some of these needs are listed above in our description of a good work environment. Others can be discovered using the following behavioral assessment tools:

- Myers-Briggs Type Indicator[25]
- DiSC Profiles[26]

---

[25] World wide web search "Myers-Briggs"
[26] TTI, Ltd., Scottsdale, Arizona

- Personality Plus[27]
- The Profile[28]

All of the above will help you gain greater understanding of the psychology that drives your behavior AND the behavior of those with whom you interact.

Gaining this knowledge is not an end in itself; you need to apply your knowledge each and every day. Knowledge is only the first step in developing a skill. As leaders, the skill we want to develop is the ability to influence our employees' behavior so that they, we and the companies we serve enjoy greater success.

There's only one way to develop skill; practice, practice, practice. It's been reported that Phil Michelson, the professional golfer, doesn't end his practice until he sinks 100 consecutive putts from a distance of three feet. Mr. Michelson knows that skills can only be developed and honed through practice.

As your leadership skills improve, the work environment you're creating improves as well. As your employees delight in an ever-improving work environment, they share their enthusiasm with your customers. The discussions above as well as in Chapter 4, *Customer Service*, have already demonstrated just how valuable your customers' experience is to your company's success in good times and bad.

---

[27] Hire Success, Indianapolis, Indiana
[28] Profiles International, Inc., Waco, Texas

Leadership is all about psychology. One of the best ways of creating a good work environment is by learning what drives your behavior and the behavior of those you employ.

Before we move on to Chapter 9, *Finance*, let's review the benefits of a good work environment.

Concept – Work Environment

> **You want your work environment to make you the employer of choice in your area while assuring your customers a pleasant experience every time they deal with your employees.**

Executive Summary – Work Environment

- Here are six things most employees want to experience in the work environment:

    o Being valued by the employer
    o Being respected and supported by peers
    o Success
    o Being recognized for success, emotionally and financially
    o Growth, personal and financial
    o Recognition that comes from teaching others to become more successful

- Other factors that influence the work environment are:

    1. Staffing
    2. Compensation
    3. Leadership

- End the cycle of overstaffing and downsizing and you'll dramatically improve your employees' perception of your work environment. It's easier than you think.

- Use compensation as an incentive rather than a reward and you'll reduce the likelihood of conflict over raises/bonuses.

- Leadership is all about psychology. Learn what drives your and your employees' behavior so that all of you can enjoy greater success.

Everything you do, every decision you make has a financial impact. Chapter 9, *Finance*, helps you understand how your decisions influence the financial results you get. Ready?

FINANCE:

Your window to the company's operations!

What you see should guide your efforts.

9

Finance

What should your finance function do for you?

Assure that your operations people have the information they need to make informed, balanced decisions.

Core Concept – Better decisions

Your company is experiencing a cash shortage. What do you do? The natural inclination is to put pressure on your collection group. Will that fix the problem? Not if your cash crunch is caused by excessive inventory, loan payments on underutilized equipment or an inflated workforce.

The knee-jerk reaction described above is all too common in business. Why? Leaders don't:

- Have the information they need to make informed decisions
- Know what information they need
- Know how to use the information available to them

Regardless of the reason, the result is that business leaders often treat symptoms rather than the disease afflicting the business. You can avoid misdiagnosing your company's ills by learning what information you need to get to the source of the problem, then using that information to make more informed and balanced decisions. That last phrase, "balanced decisions," may not be a familiar one, so let's take a moment to explore its meaning.

Balanced Decisions

Exactly what does "balanced decision" mean? A balanced decision is one that optimizes the impact a transaction has on *all three financial statements*: the balance sheet, income statement and cash flow statement. Wow, that really clarified things, didn't it? I'm kidding! That definition becomes clearer when you understand each statement's purpose. The following table should help.

Statement	Purpose
Balance sheet	Manage the resources a company owns
Income statement	Manage the profitability of a company
Cash flow statement	Manage a company's cash

As you can see these are three very different purposes, yet all are important to a company's financial health. Here's what happens when a company let's its financial situation become unbalanced:

- If a company's resources are being utilized to near capacity but they aren't generating profits, eventually some resources will have to be sold to fund the losses.
- If a company is profitable, but it's not managing its resources well, the company is likely to experience cash shortages.
- If a company's cash is managed well but it isn't generating profits, replacing expiring resources will be difficult.

To see how easily these unwanted results can occur, let's explore a common problem companies face and an even more common mistake that's made in dealing with it.

A common mistake

A company is experiencing "cash flow problems." (There is no such thing as a cash flow problem; cash shortages are symptoms of a problem, not the problem itself.) The ailing company's management decides that the way to deal with the problem is to increase sales. That makes sense. Additional sales generate additional cash, right? Ultimately, yes; *if* certain conditions are met.

First, the sales have to be profitable. If the sales aren't profitable, additional sales may actually cost you cash. If your selling price is lower than your cost, you're going to lose cash, not gain it. "Who would do that?" You'd be amazed at how many leaders operate their businesses without the information necessary to discern which of their offerings are profitable and which are not.

Second, receivables created by the additional sales must be collected. If you increase sales by selling to customers with poor credit histories, you may not collect the receivables. When that happens, you're out the cost of the product/service you delivered, exacerbating your company's cash problem.

Even if the additional sales are profitable and they are made to credit-worthy customers, the company's cash position is likely to deteriorate before it gets better. Why? Increased sales are usually accompanied by higher inventory levels. It takes cash to increase inventory and cash is already in short supply. Depending on how effectively a company's leaders manage inventory, cash could be tied up in inventory for a month or two before it's sold, then the company typically waits another 30 to 45 days to collect the receivable once the sale is made.

As you can see, increasing sales isn't a particularly effective approach to dealing with a cash shortage. Yet it's the tactic that many business leaders embrace, one of the common mistakes they make. Why? They don't have the information they need or don't know how to use the information available to them to make informed, balanced decisions.

They typically don't know which products/services are really making money for them (profitability). They don't know that their sales force is responding to a call for more sales by selling to companies with poor credit histories (cash flow management). They don't realize that inventory levels are likely to rise as sales increase (resource management). Why? They haven't explored the impact of an "increased sales" strategy on each of the financial statements. That's why it's so important that business leaders make not only informed, but balanced decisions.

*A balanced decision is one that optimizes the impact a
transaction has on all three financial statements.*

Anticipating financial impact requires an understanding of
each statement's design. Let's begin with the balance sheet.

Balance Sheet
The balance sheet is designed to show a company's financial
strength at the close of business on a specific date. The date
is the easy part; it appears at the top of the statement.
Financial strength requires further definition.

Financial Strength
The two measures we use to gauge a company's financial
strength are its liquidity and its financing risk. Liquidity is
the company's ability to pay its bills on time. Financing risk
is the amount of debt the company employs. Table 9.1
Balance Sheet Format is designed to help you visualize these
concepts as we discuss them. Let's begin with liquidity.

Liquidity
Liquidity is the company's ability to pay its bills on time.
How do we measure liquidity? We compare the company's
current assets (those assets readily convertible to cash within
12 months) with its current liabilities (the debts that come
due within 12 months). The formula is:

Current assets
Current liabilities

If the ratio is 2 to 1 or better, in other words, the company has
$2 or more of current assets (assets that can be converted to
cash in 12 months) for every $1 of current liabilities (debts
due within 12 months), its liquidity is considered good. The

Your Company
Balance Sheet
December 31, 20__

Assets (Resources owned)	Items included
Current assets	Cash, accounts receivable, inventory and prepaid expenses
Property, plant & equipment	Real estate, production equipment, vehicles, computer systems, office equipment less depreciation
Other assets	Patents, copyrights, trademarks and long-term receivables
Total Assets	
Liabilities (Debts owed)	
Current liabilities	Accounts payable, taxes (sales, payroll, income and property), wages payable & benefits owed, principal payments on loans due in the next 12 months
Long-term debt	Principal payments on loans that aren't due in the next 12 months
Other liabilities	Deposits, warranty reserves, contingency reserves
Total Liabilities	
Equity (Owners' investment)	
Common stock	The amount the stockholders invested in the business
Retained earnings	Undistributed profits less any losses incurred since the inception of the business
Total Equity	
Total Liabilities & Equity	

Table 9.1 Balance Sheet Format with line item details

company shouldn't have problems paying its bills on time. That's our first measure of financial strength. The second is financing risk.

Financing risk
Companies use a combination of debt (money they borrow) and equity (money the owners/stockholders have invested in the business) to finance the assets they own. This fact is reflected in the balance sheet equation:

$$\text{Assets} = \text{Liabilities} + \text{Equity}$$

The higher the level of debt (liabilities) in relation to the owners'/stockholders' investment (equity), the greater the financing risk. Why? Debt requires monthly payments in good times and bad.

Equity doesn't have that requirement. Companies are not required to distribute profits or return an owner's investment. The monthly cash outlays associated with debt add risk, called financing risk, to a company's operations. In ratio form, financing risk is:

$$\frac{\text{Total liabilities}}{\text{Total equity}}$$

What's a reasonable level of risk? Let's see what bankers say. They're in the business to providing debt financing.

Banks are typically comfortable with debt levels of $2.50 for every $1.00 of equity employed. When the ratio gets above 2.5/1 they get concerned. What do they fear? That the owners will walk away during difficult times leaving them holding the bag.

Here's the rationale from a banker's perspective. An owner who has $100,000 invested, but owes $1,000,000 in debt is more likely to walk away from a difficult situation than one that owes $250,000. Makes sense, doesn't it? It's easy to see how an owner facing a difficult business situation would find it easy to walk away from her $100,000 investment knowing that before she gets her $100,000 back she has to repay $1,000,000 in debt. The debt hurdle doesn't seem quite so overwhelming when she owes $250,000.

As we've just seen, the balance sheet offers two measures of financial strength, liquidity and financing risk. Before we move on to the income statement, let's talk about how the balance sheet can help us generate cash when we need it.

Financing capabilities

Two situations that every company faces are difficult times and investment opportunities. Both require cash. The key is to know how to generate cash when you need it. Here are some of the alternatives available to you:

- Use assets as collateral for loans
- Sell assets that are underutilized or absorb the excess capacity by becoming a subcontractor to other companies
- Manage your assets more effectively; i.e., collect accounts receivable on time; find ways to increase sales *without* adding inventory

Each of these alternatives is available all the time, but their effectiveness often depends on the economic situation you're facing. Let's see how the economy affects each alternative.

Collateral for loans

In an economy in which interest rates are high, you'll want to use your current assets (accounts receivable and inventory) to obtain short-term loans like a line of credit (a one-year loan). Why? When interest rates are high, they're more likely to go down than up. You want to position your company to take advantage of lower rates as they become available.

Conversely, when interest rates are low you'll want to use your real estate and equipment as collateral to obtain long-term loans to lock in the low rates.

Asset sales/subcontracting

Good economic times offer an excellent opportunity to sell under-utilized equipment and real estate at a good price. Poor economies tend to depress the value of assets. That's why subcontract work is a more viable alternative than selling equipment or real estate during difficult times.

Managing assets

Good asset management should be a part of our daily routine, good times and bad. Unfortunately, during good economic times we tend to get sloppy; we allow the average age of the receivables to climb and our inventories to become bloated. Why? Cash is being generated by the truckload despite our inattention to asset management. The fact that we've become sloppy usually doesn't hit us until the economy slows and we find our company short of cash. Good asset management pays, good times and bad.

Whether you need cash for difficult times or an investment opportunity, the three alternatives just described offer ways to generate cash using the assets listed on your balance sheet.

In essence, what I'm suggesting is that you look at your assets as pockets of cash. Each asset represents a pocket of cash. You can access the cash in that pocket by using the asset for collateral, selling it or managing the asset more effectively. By viewing your assets in this way, you'll assure that you know how to get cash when you need it.

> *Every month, view the assets on your balance sheet as pockets of cash, determine under which circumstances it makes sense to tap each pocket, then you'll have a good sense for your company's financing capabilities.*

As you can see, the balance sheet helps you evaluate your company's financial strength by highlighting its liquidity (the ability to pay its bills on time) and its financing risk (the amount of debt being employed). The balance sheet also helps you assess your company's financing capability, its ability to generate cash when needed. That's a lot of useful information from just one statement. Now, let's turn our attention to the income statement to see what it can do for us.

Income Statement

The income statement is designed to measure a company's profitability for a period of time; it's an activity report. Where the balance sheet shows a specific date, the income statement refers to a period of time. The heading will read, "For the month ending ...," "For the quarter ending ..." or "For the year ending ..." The income statement reports the company's performance, profitability, for that period of time.

The term "profit" can have different meanings depending on where it appears in the income statement. Table 9.2, Income Statement Format, includes four profit measures:

- Gross profit
- Operating income
- Income before income taxes
- Net income

Why do we have so many profit measures? To make it easier to identify what happened when the bottom line isn't what you expect, whether it's better or worse than expected.

When your company's results are better than expected, you want to know why so you can continue practices that are working well. When results are disappointing, you want to know why so that you can adjust the way your company operates. Either way, it's important to know what's causing the unexpected result. A closer look at each profit measure will help you understand how to use these measures to identify cause/effect relationships.

Gross profit
Gross profit is the profit that's left after your company has covered its production costs. In formula form, it looks like this:

$$\text{Gross profit} = \text{Sales/revenues} - \text{Cost of goods sold/Cost of sales}$$

Both "Cost of goods sold" and "Cost of sales" are terms that refer to production costs. Companies that sell products typically use "Cost of goods sold" while service companies use "Cost of sales."

"Sales" and "Revenues" are terms used to designate the income a company generates. "Sales" is used for product sales, while "Revenues" is used for service businesses. Now

Your Company
Income Statement
For the year ending December 31, 20__

	Items included
Sales/Revenues	Product sales/service revenues
Cost of goods sold/Cost of sales (cost of goods sold is used in mfg. & distribution, cost of sales for services)	Production costs – materials, labor, benefits, equipment, facilities, etc.
Gross profit	Sales/Revenues minus Cost of Goods Sold/Cost of Sales
Operating expenses (overhead): Selling expenses	Advertising, sales compensation & benefits, travel costs, trade shows
General & administrative expenses	Anything that doesn't fit into production costs or selling expenses
Total operating expenses	Selling + G&A expenses
Operating income	Gross profit minus Total operating expenses
Extraordinary gains/losses	Rare and infrequent occurrences – acts of God, plant closings, litigation settlements, downsizing costs (are these rare occurrences any more?)
Income before income taxes	Operating income +/- extraordinary gains/losses
Income taxes	Income tax expense based on income before income taxes
Net income	The profit available to the owners

Table 9.2 Income Statement Format with line item details

- Price
- Cost of production
- Capacity utilization (sales volume)

Price

If you are not achieving your gross profit targets you may not be charging enough for your offerings. How can that be when you established a profit margin target when you set your prices? Several things could have occurred.

1. Your vendors have increased their prices and you haven't passed the increase onto your customers
2. You've improved the quality of your offerings, but haven't increased your prices
3. You've added services for your customers, but you haven't built them into your pricing

You're probably wondering why prices weren't raised in each of these situations. Here's the "reason" I'm given most often when I ask that question. "I can't raise prices, my competitors won't let me."

I hope that you're not buying that answer. When business leaders are reluctant to raise prices in the three instances listed above, it's typically for the following reasons:

1. When management isn't passing along cost increases, it's usually because it feels that the company isn't serving its customers well
2. When a company improves the quality of its offerings but doesn't increase its prices, it's trying to differentiate itself from its competitors. All too often the enhanced quality isn't valued by the customer

       which is the real reason why the company can't get a
       higher price
3. Ditto number 2 when a company adds services
    without increasing prices
4. The sales force does not understand the value of the
    improved quality or additional services
5. The sales force hasn't been trained to quantify the
    value of enhanced quality/additional services for their
    customers

These are the reasons why companies don't get higher prices
for their offerings. It has nothing to do with what their
competitors are doing. As we discussed in Chapter 1,
Strategy, and Chapter 5, *Pricing*, a company should get
higher prices than its competitors *if* it's providing greater
value to the customer.

***Raising prices is an excellent way to improve both your
company's gross profit and bottom line.***

The second factor influencing gross profit is production cost.

Production costs
Are your production costs higher or lower than expected? If
they're higher, review your production processes using the
techniques in Chapter 6, *Production* to help you lower them.

If production costs are lower than expected, discover why.
Then apply what you learn to other production activities. It's
easy to overlook these opportunities because there are always
production "problems" to address. Don't fall into that trap.
As you review the income statement each month ask:

- Which activities produced better than expected results?
- Why are the results better?
- How can we duplicate this success?"

Lowering production costs requires a larger investment than raising prices, but the investment can significantly improve your company's gross profit percentage (margin).

Let's shift our attention to capacity utilization, the third factor influencing gross profit.

Capacity utilization
Capacity utilization is determined by comparing unit sales with production capacity. Let's say that your production facility is equipped to produce 1,000,000 units a month. If you're only selling 300,000 a month, your production capacity is being severely underutilized. This excess capacity results in a lot of unnecessary costs:

- Rent on excess space
- Utility costs for excess space
- Insurance costs for both the excess space and the excess equipment
- Depreciation on excess equipment
- Interest costs for carrying the excess investment
- Property taxes on the excess real estate and equipment

These excess costs, because they're considered production costs, reduce gross profit on the income statement. So, if your gross profit isn't as high as expected, the answer may be that your company has excess capacity.

Overutilization can be equally expensive. Assuming the same 1,000,000 unit capacity, if you're selling 1,100,000 million units per month, demand for your offering exceeds supply. Companies facing this situation often try to extend their capacity by working overtime and deferring equipment maintenance (especially if the sales growth is thought to be temporary). These actions create a different set of costs:

- Overtime pay
- More downtime and, ultimately, higher repair costs due to deferred maintenance
- Mistakes caused by employee fatigue
- Higher absenteeism, the need for temporary help, more workmen's compensation claims and higher insurance premiums; all of these costs are associated with employee fatigue

Capacity utilization can be expensive regardless of whether you are experiencing significant over or underutilization.

Before we move on to our second profit measure, operating income, let's review the approach that leads us to investigate pricing, production costs and capacity utilization.

First we look at the bottom line (net income) to see if it's what we expected. If it isn't, we look at the gross profit percentage to see if it's what we expected based on the profit margin built into our pricing. If it isn't, we know that there are only three factors that influence gross profit, pricing, production costs and capacity utilization. That's how we come to investigate these three factors.

What we learn during the course of our investigation will help us improve both gross profit and the bottom line (net income) in the future. I'm sure that some of you are wondering, what happens if the bottom line isn't what we expected, but gross profit is. That brings us to our second profit measure operating income.

Operating income

Operating income is calculated by subtracting operating expenses from gross profit. The formula is:

Operating income = Gross profit – Operating expenses

Gross profit was defined above. Operating expenses includes two categories of expenses, selling expenses and general & administrative expenses. What do these categories include?

Selling expenses represent all the costs associated with marketing and selling your offerings. Advertising, sales salaries and related benefit costs, sales commissions, public relations, travel, lodging, entertainment and trade show costs are all selling expenses.

General and administrative expenses are all other costs your company incurs that aren't production costs or selling expenses. This category includes administrative salaries and benefits, office facility costs, office equipment costs, office supplies, interest, business taxes/licenses, retirement plan administration, bad debts as well as accounting and legal costs. This list certainly isn't all inclusive. It's easier to define general & administrative expenses by what they are not. They are not production costs or selling expenses.

In essence, operating income is the profit we have left after we've covered production costs and overhead, selling, general & administrative expenses. If you look at the income statement format in Table 9.2 on page 246, you'll find that operating income is a profit measure that is obtained by subtracting both production costs (Cost of goods sold/Cost of sales) and operating expenses (Total selling, general & administrative expenses). The question is, "How do we use this profit measure?"

Once again, we return to the cycle of investigation described in the gross profit section. We ascertain that the bottom line isn't what we expected. The first thing we do is look at the gross profit percentage (margin) to see whether the result we achieved is the same percentage we built into our pricing. If it is, we know that our pricing, production costs and capacity utilization are on target. They're not the reasons behind our bottom line aberration.

The next step is to see whether the operating income number is what you expect. If not, you know that you need only investigate the selling, general & administrative expenses to find out why operating income isn't what you expected. How do we know that?

Using Table 9.2 on page 246, we can see that the only items between gross profit, which we ascertained is on target, and operating income are the selling, general & administrative expenses. The unexpected operating income number can only be explained by fluctuations in the selling, general & administrative expenses. That's where you need to focus your attention.

Your investigation will help you understand why these costs are out of line and what you can do to prevent this from happening in the future.

Before we move on to our next profit measure, I'd like to offer some additional insights into selling and general & administrative expenses, often referred to as overhead.

Selling expenses

You may be wondering why we separate the selling expenses from the general and administrative expenses. By listing selling expenses as a separate category, we get a sense for the return our sales and marketing efforts are generating. How? We divide sales/revenue dollars by total selling expenses.

$$\frac{\text{Sales/revenues}}{\text{Total selling expenses}}$$

This tells us how many dollars of revenue we're generating for each dollar of selling expense we've invested.

While this ratio can provide an indication of the effectiveness of your sales/marketing efforts, it is a rough measure. Why? First, marketing and sales efforts don't produce immediate results. It often takes years of marketing to create brand identity and months for a sales effort to produce results. Second, new product/service introductions often require huge marketing/selling outlays for a year or more before significant results are seen. Third, sales and marketing costs go up dramatically when a company is attempting to enter new markets.

As you can see, examining one month's return on selling expenses isn't very helpful. When examined over the course of three to five years, however, this ratio can indicate whether your company is becoming more or less adept at marketing and sales.

Overhead analysis
Now that we have a sense for what's included in the operating expenses (often referred to as overhead), how do we use this information? Here are a few questions that will help you evaluate your operating expenses.

- Are operating expenses growing faster or slower than sales/revenues? Ideally, you'd like overhead growth to lag revenue growth unless the overhead growth is related to increased R&D or new product/service introductions.
- How does revenue growth compare with the increase in selling expenses? We've already discussed the rationale behind this question in *Selling expenses* above.
- Are increased selling expenses resulting in higher gross profit? Selling expenses don't always have to result in higher sales volume. If selling expense expenditures help your sales force educate buyers in a way that allows you to improve your pricing and, consequently, your company's gross profit margin, it's a wise investment.
- What trends do you see in the general and administrative expenses you incur? Are any of them growing faster than the current inflation rate? If so, what can be done to slow their growth?
- Are you ignoring some costs because they're "fixed?" Economists tell us that in the long run, there is no such thing as a fixed cost. Investigate all expenses, even the "fixed" expenses.

Obviously, there are many more questions that can and should be asked. The questions listed above are offered as a starting point for your overhead analysis.

Overhead growth should lag revenue growth unless you're increasing your R&D investment, introducing new products/services or expanding into new markets.

Remember, when you're trying to discover why the bottom line isn't what you expected, begin with gross profit. If that's in line with the margin you targeted in your pricing, turn your attention to operating income. If operating income isn't what you expect, investigate your operating expenses, the selling, general & administrative expenses.

What do you do when both gross profit and operating income are what you expected, but the bottom line isn't? Look to the third profit measure, income before income taxes.

Income before income taxes
Table 9.2 - Income Statement Format shows us that there is only one category that separates operating income from income before income taxes. That category is extraordinary gains/losses.

Income before income taxes is calculated by adding extraordinary gains and subtracting extraordinary losses from operating income. The formula looks like this:

Income before =   Operating income
income taxes   +Extraordinary gains
                     - Extraordinary losses

If operating income is what you expect but the bottom line isn't, it's likely that your company is experiencing extraordinary gains or losses. What are extraordinary gains/losses? Let's take a look.

Extraordinary gains/losses
Extraordinary gains and losses represent financial results that stem from rare and infrequent occurrences. The types of things that you'll see included in this category are:

- Gains/losses associated with acts of God, fires, floods, earthquakes, etc.
- Litigation settlements
- Gain/loss on sale of real estate, equipment and other assets included in the Property, Plant & Equipment category on the balance sheet
- Costs associated with plant closings
- Cost of termination/early retirement packages associated with downsizings (I'm not sure that these qualify as "rare and infrequent" anymore; the financial community is discussing the possibility of requiring that these costs be included in operating expenses in the future to reflect the level of control management has over these decisions)

You may be wondering why extraordinary gains are not included in sales/revenues and why extraordinary losses aren't listed with operating expenses. The answer lies in the purpose behind the income statement.

Income statement purpose
The income statement is designed to help us measure profits, the company's performance, over a period of time. The income statement's greatest value comes from comparing

results from multiple years. Why? This comparison enables us to discern trends in profitability. Trends in sales, gross profit and overhead costs help us understand whether we're getting better or worse at managing our operations.

If the results of rare and infrequent occurrences (extraordinary gains/losses) were included in with normal operating results, it would be more difficult to determine whether our management skills are improving or declining. That's the reason why we list extraordinary gains/losses in a separate section of the income statement. That's why we separate them from the results of normal operating activities.

Separating extraordinary gains/losses from normal operating results allows us to more readily discern trends in our company's normal operations.

Income before income taxes also allows us to determine what the company's average income tax rate is. Given the complexity of today's tax laws and their ever-changing nature, it's often difficult for the lay person to know whether or not a company is managing its tax expense well. Having said that, I believe it's still worth knowing how you can calculate a company's average tax rate. Here's the formula:

$$\frac{\text{Income taxes}}{\text{Income before income taxes}}$$

If you're really interested in the tax implications of operating decisions, here are a few questions that can help you start the conversation with your accountants.

- Why did income taxes go down when profits are up?
- Why do we show a tax benefit (anticipated refund) when we have profits?
- Why do we owe income taxes when we have a loss?

Income taxes are subtracted from income before income taxes to get to the bottom line, our fourth profit measure.

Net income
Net income, often referred to as the bottom line, is the profit that's available to the owners of the business. How do you calculate net income? Here's the formula:

Net income = Income before income taxes – Income taxes

While it's mathematically accurate, that formula doesn't do justice to what net income really represents. Net income is the profit that's left after the company has covered all production costs (cost of goods sold/cost of sales), all overhead costs (selling, general & administrative expenses), extraordinary items and income taxes. That's a mouthful!

Let's see if Table 9.3 – Profit Measure Comparison makes it easier to understand what's included in net income as well as the other three profit measures we discussed. *Note: IBIT in the table below represents income before income taxes.*

What we can see from this table is that the gross profit is the profit the company has after covering productions costs (cost of goods sold/cost of sales). Operating income is the profit that's left after covering both production costs and overhead (selling, general & admin. costs). IBIT is the profit left after covering production costs, overhead and extraordinary items.

	Gross profit	Operating income	IBIT	Net income
Sales/revenues	included	included	included	included
Cost of goods sold/cost of sales	included	included	included	included
Gross profit	included	included	included	included
Selling, general & admin. costs		included	included	included
Operating income		included	included	included
Extraordinary gains/losses			included	included
IBIT			included	included
Income taxes				included
Net income				included

Table 9.3 – Profit Measure Comparison.

Net income is the profit available to the owners after all revenues and costs are considered. Again, the reason for having so many profit measures is to help you narrow your focus to a few issues when the bottom line isn't what you expect it to be.

The income statement is designed to measure a company's performance (profitability) for a period of time.

With the balance sheet and income statement under our belts, it's time to turn our attention to the third financial statement, the cash flow statement. Let's see what it can do for us.

Cash Flow Statement

The cash flow statement was created in response to the
question, "If we're making this much money, where's the
cash?" This question indicates that business owners/leaders
doubt the profit numbers they're seeing. Why? They're
expecting these profits to appear as additional cash on the
balance sheet and it isn't happening.

How does the cash flow statement deal with this dilemma? It
shows all of the sources and uses of cash during the period in
question. Like the income statement, the cash flow statement
is an activity report. The heading for both statements reads
"For the month ending…," "For the quarter ending…" or
"For the year ending…." While both statements are activity
reports, the cash flow statement's focus is cash, while the
income statement's focus is profits.

As you can see in Table 9.4 – Cash Flow Statement Format,
there are three major categories in the cash flow statement,
operating activities, investing activities and financing
activities. Let's see what these categories tell us about how
cash is being managed.

Operating activities

The operating activities section shows how much cash your
company is generating from profits. In order to understand
how this works, we need to take a little detour. We need to
discuss the two most commonly used methods of accounting,
the cash method and the accrual method. These accounting
methods define how profits are calculated.

Your Company
Cash Flow Statement
For the year ending December 31, 20__

OPERATING ACTIVITIES	Items included
Net income	Bottom line of income statement
Add: depreciation & amortization	Non-cash expenses shown in income statement
Add/subtract: Changes in current assets other than cash and current liabilities other than the revolving line of credit and current portion of long-term debt	Changes in current asset accounts (from balance sheet) current liability accounts (from balance sheet) except as noted in column 1
Net cash from operating activities	Total of all items listed above
INVESTING ACTIVITIES	
Purchases/sales of long-term assets	Purchase/sale of property, equipment, copyrights, patents, trademarks, stocks (including subsidiary companies), joint ventures and bonds
Net cash from investing activities	The total of all items appearing in Investing activities
FINANCING ACTIVITIES	
Borrowing/loan repayments	Cash generated from new loans or used to repay old loans
Owner investments/distributions	Cash invested by owners or cash distributed to owners
Dividends paid	Profits distributed to owners
Net cash from financing activities	The total of all financing activities
Net increase (decrease in cash)	The total of all three categories – operating, investing and financing activities
Cash – beginning of the period	From previous balance sheet
Cash – end of the period	Should agree with cash shown on current balance sheet

Table 9.4 - Cash Flow Statement Format with details

Cash method

The cash method of accounting states that nothing gets recorded on the books until cash changes hands. That means income isn't recorded until cash is received and expenses aren't recorded until bills are paid.

There are two exceptions to the rule that nothing is recorded until cash changes hands. Those two exceptions are depreciation and amortization expense. These two expenses represent paper entries; i.e., no cash changes hands when these expenses are recorded. Why? Depreciation and amortization represent the loss in value of long-term assets like real estate, equipment, patents, copyrights and trademarks. Here's how depreciation and amortization work.

When a company buys a long-term asset, it realizes that the asset will benefit multiple years. Real estate might be used for 40 or 50 years, equipment 3 to 15 years, patents offer 17 years protection, and so on. Investments in these long-term assets are made with the expectation of generating returns (profits) throughout the life of the asset. With that goal in mind, it isn't fair to charge the month or year in which the asset is purchased with its total cost. What we do instead is record the investment as an asset.

Real estate and equipment are listed in the balance sheet, Table 9.1 - Balance Sheet, in a category called "Property, plant and equipment." Patents, copyrights and trademarks are included in "Other Assets." These investments typically lose value over time.

The tangible assets (property, plant and equipment) lose value through use and age. Real estate might be an exception if it is in a prime location. Since there are many factors (location, interest rates, occupancy rates, amount of space coming onto the market) that influence real estate values, we treat real estate like any other long-term asset and expect it to lose value. This loss in value is called depreciation expense. It is recorded monthly over the life of the asset by reducing the value of the asset in the balance sheet and showing that loss as an expense in the income statement. As you can see, this is a paper entry; no cash is changing hands.

Similarly, intangible assets like patents, copyrights and trademarks lose value over time. For these assets, the loss of value relates to the expiration of a right. These intangible assets give you the right to protect your company's creations from use by others.   Each month a portion of that right expires and the asset itself is less valuable. We record that loss in value in the same way we do with tangible assets; we reduce the value of the asset on the balance sheet and record the expense in the income statement. The loss of value of intangible assets is called amortization expense. Neither depreciation nor amortization involves cash changing hands.

Since both depreciation and amortization are expenses involved in calculating profit in the income statement and neither involves an exchange of cash at the time the expense is recorded, we add them back to net income to determine how much cash was generated from profits. In essence, a company that has depreciation and amortization expenses is generating more cash than profits.

Some of you are probably wondering why the cash used to acquire these assets and the monthly loan payments on these assets are not included in cash flow from operating activities. Cash expended to acquire assets is shown in "Investing

Activities." Monthly loan payments are reflected in "Financing Activities." The reasons will become clear as you read those sections.

I'm sure you're wondering why you need to understand the cash method of accounting with all of its idiosyncrasies in order to understand cash flow from operating activities. That will be easier to see when you can see how the accrual method differs from the cash method. Let's see what those differences are.

Accrual method

The accrual method of accounting requires that income be recorded on the books at the time it is earned and expenses when they're incurred (when the company becomes liable for them). An exchange of cash is *not* required for income or expenses to be recorded on the books.

What that means is that when we make a sale, we record it immediately even though we might not be paid for 30 to 45 days or more. We accomplish this by recording an account receivable on the balance sheet reflecting the fact that we are owed money by our customers and recording the sale on the income statement.

Similarly, we record production costs and many of the selling, general & administrative expenses by recording the vendor's invoice when it's received even though it hasn't been paid. The amount of the vendor's invoice appears as an account payable on the balance sheet to indicate that we owe the money and as a production cost, selling expense or general & administrative expense on the income statement.

Some expenses like payroll, payroll taxes, 401(k) matching and income taxes are not invoiced; yet these expenses need to be recorded on the books in the period in which they are incurred (when we become liable for them). These non-invoiced expenses are called accrued expenses. Again, the liability for accrued expenses is shown on the balance sheet while the expense itself appears in the income statement as production cost, selling expense or general & administrative expense, depending upon the nature of the expense.

Since receivables are often collected months after the sale is recorded and payables/accrued expenses are paid in months following their recording, we have a significant timing difference between profits and cash flow. This difference requires that all income and expense items in the income statement be adjusted to reflect the actual exchange of cash to determine how much cash is generated from profits. Let's see what those adjustments are.

Accrual method adjustments
The operating activities section for a company using the accrual method begins with net income. To that we add the non-cash expenses of depreciation and amortization just as we did under the cash method of accounting. Our next step is to adjust for changes in current assets and current liabilities. Why? Transactions that affect most current asset and current liability accounts also affect the income statement. Here's how it works.

Current assets include cash, accounts receivable, inventory and prepaid expenses. We don't make an adjustment for cash in the operating activities section because cash is being affected by transactions in all three categories of the cash flow statement, operating activities, investing activities and financing activities. We do make adjustments for accounts receivable, inventory and prepaid expenses.

- Accounts receivable are created when sales are made; sales are reported in the income statement.
- Inventory is reduced when an item is shipped and the cost of that item is transferred to cost of goods sold/cost of sales in the income statement.
- Prepaid expenses represent expenses paid in advance of receiving the benefit. Insurance and maintenance costs are two examples of expenses paid in advance. These costs are set up as a current asset when paid, then expensed over the one-year term these policies and contracts typically cover. Each month prepaid expense is reduced on the balance sheet by a prorata amount ($1/12^{th}$ of a 12 month contract) and expensed in the income statement.

Similarly, all current liabilities other than a company's revolving line of credit and current portion of long-term debt are related to the income statement. As mentioned earlier, accounts payable and accrued expenses are created by incurring production costs, selling expenses and general & administrative expenses. All of these accrued costs/expenses appear in the income statement.

The only two current liabilities that don't relate directly to the income statement are the revolving line of credit and the current portion of long-term debt. A revolving line of credit is a loan, typically from a bank, that has a one-year term. It's very similar to your home equity credit line. You draw funds as you need them and repay as you have cash available. The only thing you have to pay monthly is the interest. The funds from this type of loan can be used for any purpose including asset purchases. Asset purchases are not reflected in the income statement. That's why we don't include the revolving line of credit in the operating activities section.

The current portion of long-term debt represents the principal portion of loan payments due in the next twelve months. The phrase, current portion, means due in the next twelve months. Long-term debt refers to any debt that has a maturity of more than one year. While the interest portion of each payment is expensed in the income statement, the principal portion of the payment reduces liabilities in the balance sheet. Since the principal portion of the payment does not affect the income statement, the payments are not included as accrual method adjustments. They appear later in "Financing Activities."

The purpose of accrual method adjustments is to convert accrual method profits to cash method profits.

Visually, here's how cash method and accrual method differ.

CASH METHOD	ACCRUAL METHOD
Operating Activities: Net income + depreciation & amortization	**Operating Activities:** Net income + depreciation & amortization +/- accts receivable change +/- inventory change +/- prepaid expense changes +/- accts payable change +/- accrued expense changes
Net cash flow from *operating activities*	*Net cash flow from* *operating activities*

Table 9.5 – Cash Method/Accrual Method Comparison

As you can see, there's a lot more involved in calculating cash flow from profits (operating activities) under the accrual method than there is under the cash method.

Under the cash method of accounting, all items in the income statement represent cash transactions *except* depreciation and amortization. To determine how much cash was generated from profits, simply add the depreciation and amortization expenses to net income. That's the only adjustment you need to make.

With the accrual method you not only add back depreciation and amortization, you consider the changes in the current asset and current liability accounts listed above in Table 9.5.

Why choose the accrual method with its complexity? For many companies the accrual method offers a more accurate picture of their profitability.

The cash method of accounting does a good job of measuring profits for businesses that get paid when the product/service is delivered. Restaurants, appliance repair people, towing services, locksmiths, residential cleaning services and lawn services are all businesses for which the cash method of accounting works well. Income is received in cash at the time the product/service is provided and the costs are paid within a few days or week after the cost is incurred. It's the proximity in time of both revenue and cost cash flows that allows the cash method to accurately reflect a company's profits. That's not true for the majority of businesses.

Many businesses wait 30 to 45 days or more to get paid for the revenues they generate. Similarly, they wait 30 to 45 days or more to pay for the costs they incur. In situations like this, the accrual method does a better job of measuring profits by ignoring the exchange of cash. Instead, revenues are recorded when earned and costs/expenses when incurred (when the company becomes liable for them).

While many business leaders get a more accurate profit picture from the accrual method, they lose sight of what's happening with cash. That's why the cash flow statement was created and why we convert profits to cash flow in the operating activities section of the cash flow statement.

The Operating Activities section of the cash flow statement represents the amount of cash generated from profits.

We've covered operating activities, the first and most complicated section of the cash flow statement. It's time to move on to investing activities. Before we do, I want to assure you that the cash flow statement gets much easier from this point forward.

Investing Activities
Cash flow from investing activities deals with the investment in and sale of non-current assets, in other words, any asset included in the property, plant and equipment and other asset categories in the balance sheet.

If you purchase an asset in one of these categories, cash goes down. Conversely, selling these assets increases cash. Net cash from investing activities is the sum of all cash generated by sales of non-current assets less amounts expended to purchase assets. That's all there is to cash flow from investing activities. I told you it would get easier.

The Investing Activities section of the cash flow statement reflects cash generated from the sale of long-term assets and cash invested in acquiring long-term assets.

Now, let's move onto the third section of the cash flow statement, financing activities.

Financing Activities

Cash generated through financing activities comes from loans (debt financing) or owner investment (equity financing). Cash is used in financing activities to repay debt or distribute money back to the owners.

Debt financing activities are easy to visualize. Cash is generated when money is borrowed. Cash is used when loans are repaid. How do you know whether a company is borrowing money or repaying debt? Look at the balance sheet. Specifically, look at whether the revolving line of credit and current portion of long-term debt items in current liabilities have increased or decreased since the last balance sheet date.

An increase indicates that the company is borrowing money; a decrease means the company is repaying debt. Now, make that same period-to-period comparison for the items in long-term debt section of the balance sheet. What you'll find is that some items of debt increase while others decrease. It's important that each item of debt appear separately in the financing activities section so that you know how the mix of debt financing is changing. You'll gain more insights into the importance of separate listings in the section entitled Cash flow analysis below.

Equity financing activity is found in the balance sheet in the equity section. Compare the owners' account balances with the previous balance sheet's balances to see whether they're increasing or decreasing.

Owners' accounts in sole proprietorships and partnerships are called owner's capital. In corporations, they appear under the names common stock, additional paid-in capital and treasury stock. In limited liability companies, they're called member balances or member accounts.

Investments in the business are reflected as increases in owners' capital, common stock, additional paid-in capital or members' balances. Distributions to proprietors and partners are reflected as decreases in owners' capital. Distributions in limited liability companies reduce members' balances. It's the same activity, just different account names.

In a corporation the same distributions are occurring, but we give them different names. If the company buys back its own stock (a distribution), the amount paid appears as an increase in treasury stock. It's called treasury stock because the stock is returned to the treasury for future reissuance.

Treasury stock is shown as a negative amount in the equity section on the balance sheet because it represents a reduction in stockholder investments in the company. Stock buybacks are only one form of distribution; the other is a distribution of profits called dividends.

When a company pays a dividend it distributes profits to the stockholders. Retained earnings, on the balance sheet, is reduced by the amount of the dividend. Both types of cash distributions, stock buybacks and dividends use cash.

Let's recap the financing activities section. Increases in equity accounts (other than treasury stock) reflect additional investment in the business which means cash is coming into the business. Decreases in equity accounts (other than treasury stock) indicate that cash is being distributed to the owners. These distributions result in a reduction in cash.

You'll notice that I've listed treasury stock as an exception twice in the preceding paragraph. Since treasury stock represents a reduction in stockholder investment, it has a negative balance. Mathematically, that means the signs are the opposite of those described for the other equity financing activities. In other words, an increase in treasury stock (the company is buying back its own stock) means cash is going out. A decrease in treasury stock (the company is reissuing its own stock) means that cash is coming into the company.

When we add the increases and decreases in debt financing and equity financing activities we arrive at a net increase or decrease in cash from financing activities.

If I were in your shoes, I'd be wondering, "How does this information help me make better decisions?" Good question. Let's see how we can use this information once we get it.

Cash Flow Analysis
The operating activities section is at the top of the statement for a reason. A company cannot fund long-term growth unless it is able to generate cash from profits. As we explore cash flow from operating activities, we're searching for answers to the following three questions:

1. Are there any signs of operating difficulties in the operating activities section?

2. If the company is generating positive cash flow from operating activities, how is it using that cash?
3. If the company is using cash in operating activities (a negative cash flow from operating activities), how is it funding this additional cash requirement?

Some factors to consider in answering these questions are:

Operating difficulty
If a company is consistently losing money (its net income number is regularly negative), obviously there is a problem with operations. To find the source of the problem use the income statement analysis techniques described in the *Income Statement* section above.

Profitability isn't the only factor to consider when searching for operating difficulties. The way in which a company manages the current assets and current liabilities that appear in the operating activities section are important as well. Let's explore some of the more common problems business leaders encounter.

1. Let's assume that a company is experiencing negative cash flow from operating activities (it's using cash in its operations). Your investigation reveals that the accounts receivable have increased dramatically. Is this good or bad? The answer to this question is always, "It depends."

    An increase in accounts receivable due to higher than usual sales volume (assuming normal pricing and credit terms), is a good thing. The cash will be received in another month or so. If the reason why accounts receivable increased is because the company was lax in its collection efforts, that's bad.

2. Again, let's assume the company's cash flow from operating activities is negative. This time accounts receivable is fine, but the company's inventory has increased dramatically. Good or bad?

    If management increased inventory to gear up for their busy season, no problem. If the company is coming out of its busy season and inventory is growing, that's a problem.

3. This time we'll assume that the company is experiencing a positive cash flow from operating activities. The reason is that the accounts receivable is down significantly. If the decline represents collections made on receivables from an unusually high sales month, no problem. Trace the reason to several months of poor sales and you know its time to visit your customers to see what's happening.

4. The same positive cash flow scenario, this time it's because inventory is down dramatically. If inventory is down because the company is coming out of its busy season, that's good management. If the decline is due to write-offs for technological obsolescence, expired shelf life or theft, management is asleep at the wheel. Similarly, a drop in inventory for a company going into its busy season raises questions about management's attention to business.

5. Again, cash flow from operating activities is positive. This time it's because accounts payable and accrued

expense liabilities are rising significantly. If their increase is due to an increase in sales volume, no problem. If they're increasing because the company isn't paying its bills on time, the company might be facing nasty consequences including late charges, withheld shipments and higher prices (vendors often raise prices to cover their interest cost when carrying customers for extended periods of time).

As you can see, there are a variety of signs available to help you spot difficulties in a company's operations. This is, however, only the first step in the process. It's time to see how management is using the company's cash flow from operating activities.

Positive cash flow from operating activities

If a company generates positive cash flow from operating activities, how did it use that cash? There are three possibilities.

1. The company could invest the money. The amount and type of investments appear in the investing activities section of the cash flow statement.
2. The cash could be used to pay down debt, return some of the owners' investment or distribute profits to the owners. These cash outlays appear in financing activities in the cash flow statement.
3. The company could simply hang onto the cash. If it does, the ending cash balance shown in the cash flow statement will be higher than the beginning balance.

Many companies employ a combination of the above alternatives in utilizing the cash they create. The question is did they make the right choices given the consistency of their profits, cash flow and the strength of their balance sheet?

Investing cash flow from operating activities in long-term assets may be a good strategy if your company consistently produces significant amounts of cash from profits. If it doesn't, you ought to borrow the money you need to finance the investment to avoid cash shortages in the future.

Similarly, using operating activity cash flow to accelerate debt repayment, return owners' investments or distribute profits is fine if you are consistently generating cash from operating activities. If not, just make the normal loan payments, use long-term debt to finance a return of owners' investment if necessary and avoid distributing profits to owners unless required.

Now let's look at the flip side of the coin. How can management fund negative cash flows from operating activities? Let's see.

Negative cash flow from operating activities
How has management funded the negative cash flow from operating activities? Again, there are three possibilities.

1. The company can sell assets to fund the cash shortfall. If it does, the amount received and type of asset sold will appear in the Investing Activities section.
2. The company can borrow money or get existing or new investors to invest in the company. Cash gained from these activities appear in Financing Activities.
3. The company can use some of its existing cash reserves. If management uses this alternative, the

ending cash balance in the cash flow statement will be lower than the beginning cash balance.

These alternatives beg the same question we had in the positive cash flow situation, "Did management make the right choices?"

Selling long-term assets like equipment to fund negative cash flows from operating activities makes sense only if the company has significant excess capacity or the equipment has limited future use. Absent these conditions, the company could be damaging its future by selling equipment.

Similarly, selling investments in stocks or bonds when the market for them is down isn't advisable when the company has the ability to borrow the funds at a reasonable rate.

An alternative to selling assets is borrowing money to fund the shortfall. When interest rates are high or cash shortages are viewed as temporary, short-term loans work well in funding cash shortages. Low rates or long-term cash needs suggest the use of longer term loans. Of course, management must be able to demonstrate the company has the financial strength and profits necessary to support the higher levels of debt or banks won't lend them the money they need.

When selling assets and borrowing money don't make sense, you might want to find investors to fund the shortfall. I assure you that finding investors for your business is one of the most difficult things you'll ever do, especially if you own or manage a closely-held business. Getting additional equity investment from new investors is time-consuming, expensive and often unsuccessful. Why? In closely-held companies there are only a few owners which means there isn't a ready market should one of the owners need to sell. That risk alone is enough to dissuade all but the most aggressive investors.

Well established, publicly-traded companies like GE, Merck and Intel don't have this problem. For them the decision to use equity financing vs. debt financing is a matter of cost unless they're acquiring another company. Acquisitions typically involve the transfer of stock, in part, because stock doesn't require monthly cash payments like debt does.

Another option for companies experiencing negative cash flows from operating activities is fund the negative cash flow from cash reserves. This is the quickest alternative of those available. There are two factors to consider before deciding whether using cash reserves is appropriate.

First, is the negative cash flow from operating activities expected to be short-lived? If your expectation is that it will only last a month or two and your company will still have a healthy reserve at the end of that time, by all means use your cash reserve. When you expect more than two months of shortfall or your reserves are already limited, borrowing is probably a better alternative.

As you can see, the cash flow statement offers tremendous insights into the company's operations *and* management's decision-making process. The power of the cash flow statement stems from the fact that it captures every transaction in which the company is involved. That's not true of the other two statements.

The balance sheet is affected only if an asset is bought or sold, money is borrowed or repaid or the owners make an additional investment or have their investment returned to them. The income statement includes income and expenses, nothing concerning assets, liabilities or equity. The cash flow statement considers all these factors in determining how cash is generated and used.

Now that we have a sense for how to use financial statements to analyze a company's financial situation, let's explore another financial tool, ratio analysis, to see what other insights are available to us.

Financial Ratios

Financial ratios are simply another way of looking at the numbers that appear in the financial statements. They offer additional perspectives that enhance your understanding of the company's operations and help you set its direction for the future. Before I explain how that happens, let's get an overview of ratios.

There are four categories of financial ratios. Each category has a different focus as shown below.

Category	Focus
Liquidity ratios	Ability to pay bills on time
Leverage ratios	Use of debt financing
Profitability ratios	Company's profitability
Return ratios	Rates of return generated

As we explore each category in detail, you'll see how ratios help you evaluate prior results and determine where you need to focus your attention in the future. Let's begin with the liquidity ratios.

Liquidity ratios

There are four liquidity ratios:

1. Quick ratio
2. Current ratio
3. Average days sales outstanding ratio
4. Inventory turnover ratio

Quick ratio

The quick ratio helps you determine how well a company can
pay its bills on time using its most liquid assets, those that
can be converted to cash in two months or less. The ratio
looks like this:

$$\frac{\text{Cash + Marketable securities + Accounts receivable}}{\text{Current liabilities}}$$

Cash is immediately available to pay bills; marketable
securities can be converted to cash in a matter of days;
accounts receivable are typically collected in 30 to 45 days.

By comparing the quick assets to current liabilities (the debt
that comes due in the next twelve months) you get a sense for
how easily a company can meet its obligations in the next
year using only its most liquid assets. If the quick ratio is 1
to 1 (a dollar of quick assets for each dollar of current
liabilities owed) or better, the company can readily pay its
bills on time. Now, let's explore the current ratio.

Current ratio

The difference between the quick and current ratios lies in the
numerator. In the current ratio, you're including more assets
than you did with the quick ratio. The current ratio is:

$$\frac{\text{Current assets}}{\text{Current liabilities}}$$

Current assets include cash, accounts receivable, inventory and prepaid expenses. The greatest difference between quick assets and current assets is typically inventory. Prepaid expenses are typically insignificant when compared to inventory.

As with the quick ratio, you're comparing assets to current liabilities. The target for the current ratio is 2 to 1 (two dollars of current assets for every dollar of current liabilities owed) or better. Why is the current ratio target so much higher than the quick ratio? It takes more time to convert inventory to cash than it does to convert quick assets to cash.

A final note before moving on to Average Day's Sales Outstanding; the reason you want a quick ratio of 1 to 1 or better is so that you don't have to discount your prices to convert inventory to cash quickly. If a company's quick ratio is .75 to 1, it may very well have to lower its prices to accelerate the conversion of inventory to cash. Obviously, lower prices result in a lower gross profit margin and, ultimately, a smaller net income. I know that's not what you want for your company.

Average day's sales outstanding ratio
With this ratio we're calculating the average age of the accounts receivable. The ratio looks like this:

> Accounts receivable
> Sales for the period/Days included in the period

In the denominator, you're calculating the average amount of sales per day. If a company's sales for the month total $30,000, you divide the $30,000 by 30 days to arrive at a $1,000 average day's sales. The average day's sales is then divided into the accounts receivable to ascertain how many days worth of sales remain uncollected (outstanding).

The target for Average Day's Sales Outstanding varies widely by industry. Here are a few industry examples:

Food	20 to 30 days
Construction	45 to 60 days
Health Care	120 to 180 days

For most industries the norm is 30 to 45 days. These time frames tend to lengthen during difficult economic times.

You may be wondering why Average Day's Sales Outstanding is part of the liquidity group. If you refer back to the quick and current ratios, you'll see that accounts receivable is a component of both ratios. Knowing the average age of the receivables will help you evaluate the quality of the quick and current ratios. Here's how it works.

If the company's Average Day's Sales Outstanding is 38 days and the industry average is 42 days, you can feel comfortable that the receivables are likely to be collected. The quality of the accounts receivable enhances your perception of the strength of the quick and current ratios you're seeing.

Conversely, if the Average Day's Sales Outstanding is 55 days and the industry average is 42, your comfort level just dropped. Why? You can't help but wonder whether all of the accounts receivable will be collected. You know that the older a receivable gets the less likely it is to be collected. You'll see a similar pattern in our next ratio, the inventory turnover ratio.

Inventory turnover ratio

The inventory turnover ratio measures a company's effectiveness in managing its inventory. The formula is:

$$\frac{\text{Annualized cost of goods sold}}{\text{Average inventory}}$$

In the numerator we're listing the cost of the product sold. For manufacturing businesses that means the cost of producing the product; for distribution businesses, it means the cost of acquiring, storing and handling products sold. Regardless of the type of costs included, you are comparing the annualized cost of goods sold to the average inventory level maintained.

You may be wondering about the term "annualized" in the previous sentence. If the income statement you're using to calculate this ratio is for a time period less than a year, you need to annualize the cost of goods sold. How do we do this? You divide the cost of goods sold by the number of months covered by the income statement; then multiply by 12 to get an estimate of the annual cost of goods sold. The formula looks like this:

$$\frac{\text{Cost of goods sold}}{\text{Number of months in income statement}} \times 12$$

Why do you annualize the Cost of Goods Sold? One of the things you hope to learn from the inventory turnover ratio is how many times during the course of a year a company buys, sells and replaces its inventory. Unless the cost of goods sold number represents an annual number, you can't make that determination. That's the reason for annualizing the cost of goods sold.

The denominator of the inventory turnover ratio is average inventory. Here you're using a simple average:

$$\frac{\text{Beginning inventory + Ending inventory}}{2}$$

The target for most companies is 4 to 6 times a year. In other words a company will buy, sell and replace its inventory 4 times (every 3 months) to 6 times (every two months) during the course of the year. What does inventory turnover rate have to do with liquidity? What relevance does it have?

If you refer back to the current ratio, you'll recall that inventory was a significant component in the equation. Knowing how effectively a company is managing its inventory can enhance or diminish your perception of its current ratio and, thus, its ability to pay its bills on time.

Let's say that your company's inventory turnover ratio is 5 times per year and the industry average 6 times a year. The fact that your company is turning (buying, selling and replacing) inventory less frequently than is typical for its industry indicates a potential for greater inventory losses. These losses may come in the form of expired shelf life or technological obsolescence. Whenever you see an inventory turnover rate lower than the industry average, you should be asking, "Are there any items included in inventory that should be written off or written down in value?"

In addition to the loss potential, slow-moving inventory invites concerns about its value and salability. These concerns create further doubts about whether the current ratio is really as strong as it appears. Here's the thought process.

Even if the inventory can be sold, how long will it take to get rid of it and at what price? If you can't sell it quickly or you have to dramatically lower your prices, you're not likely to generate the amount of cash you need to cover your bills. If that's the situation your company is facing, then your current ratio may not be as strong as it appears.

The opposite is true as well. When your company's inventory turnover rate is higher than the industry average, there is less likelihood of inventory write-offs or write-downs; consequently, your perception of your company's current ratio is strengthened.

Liquidity ratios are designed to help you assess a company's ability to pay its bills on time.

That brings us to our second set of ratios, leverage ratios.

Leverage ratios
Leverage ratios deal with the use of debt. Leverage may seem like a strange term to associate with debt, but in reality it describes very well why debt is used.

During strong economic times (periods of high demand for your offerings), the use of debt allows your company to expand its production efforts to meet demand. Additional sales create additional profits which, in turn, increase owners' returns. In this regard, debt is said to leverage up the returns to owners. That's why the term, leverage, is used to refer to debt-related ratios.

Unfortunately, leverage works both ways. While it can leverage up profits during good times, it can lower them during difficult times. Remember, the interest cost associated with debt continues even though your company's revenues and profit margins decline.

Debt, because it often requires monthly payments, increases your company's need for cash. During good times, that may not be a problem, but during periods of declining sales your company may have difficulty making its payments.

The leverage ratios are:

1. Debt to equity ratio
2. Debt service coverage ratio
3. Times interest earned ratio

Debt to equity ratio
This ratio shows the mix of debt and equity being used to finance the business. The formula is:

Total liabilities
Total owners' equity (stockholders' equity in corporations)

This ratio offers us a couple of insights. First, it helps us assess the company's financing risk; typically, the higher the level of debt the greater the risk. Why? Debt requires monthly cash payments, good times and bad; equity does not.

The second thing that we can surmise from the debt to equity ratio is the company's borrowing capacity. Many banks will lend up to about 2.5 to 1 ($2.50 of debt for every dollar the owners have invested in the business). A company with a debt to equity ratio of less than 2.5 to 1 usually is considered to have additional borrowing capacity.

When the debt to equity ratio rises above 2.5 to 1, the likelihood of getting a loan drops, indicating diminished borrowing capacity. Obviously, it's important to know what your company's odds are for getting a loan when it needs it.

Does the fact that a company has additional borrowing capacity indicate that it should borrow more money? The debt service coverage ratio helps us answer that question.

Debt service coverage ratio
While the debt to equity ratio deals with borrowing capacity; the debt service coverage ratio deals with the affordability of debt. In essence, the debt service coverage ratio tells you whether a company is generating enough profits to afford the level of debt it has or desires. The formula you use to make that determination is:

$$\frac{\text{Income before income taxes} + \text{interest expense}}{\text{Current portion of long-term debt} + \text{interest expense}}$$

Before we tackle the formula, let's explore the meaning of "debt service coverage." "Debt service" refers to the principal and interest payments a company must make. In the formula above, the debt service is calculated in the denominator; it is the current portion of long-term debt + interest expense.

Current portion of long-term debt represents the principal payments due in the next twelve months. Interest expense represents the interest costs for the past twelve months or projected for the next twelve months whichever is easier to obtain. When combined, the current portion of long-term debt and interest expense equal the company's debt service requirement for the coming year.

In the numerator, you're calculating the profit available to pay the debt service. You begin with the income before income taxes and add back interest expense. Why?

Income before income taxes represents the profit a company earns after it has covered production costs, overhead and extraordinary items. Interest expense is usually included in the overhead which means that income before income taxes represents profit *after* interest expense. What you're trying to ascertain in this formula is the profit available *before* interest expense. That's why we add back interest expense to income before income taxes in calculating the profit available to cover debt service.

A math question I often get is, "Why don't you just cancel the interest expense since it appears in both the numerator and denominator?" The answer is that the math rules don't allow us to cancel items when we're adding or subtracting them, only when we're multiplying or dividing. Since interest is being added in the numerator and denominator, we can't cancel them.

The target we have for the debt service coverage ratio is 1.25 to 1 ($1.25 of profit for every dollar of debt service we're required to pay). This target not only tells us how well a company is covering its debt, but it can help us determine how much additional debt service it can afford. Here's how it works.

A company wants to upgrade its production facilities. To do so, it'll have to borrow $20 million dollars and the monthly debt service (principal and interest payment) on that loan will be $415,000. To determine whether its current profits are adequate to handle the additional debt service, simply add

$4,980,000 (415,000 x 12 months) to the existing debt service shown in the denominator and recalculate the debt service coverage ratio. If the ratio is still 1.25 to 1 or better, the additional debt service should be manageable. If the ratio drops below 1.25 to 1, you may want to reevaluate your decision to make the investment or how you finance it.

The third leverage ratio, Times Interest Earned, comes into play when the Debt Service Coverage ratio is marginal.

Times interest earned ratio

Let's say that a company's debt service coverage ratio is 1 to 1 (one dollar of profit for every dollar of debt payment). If anything goes wrong, the economy declines or competition increases, this company may have trouble making its monthly payments. If that happens, management may need to go to the bank with a plan to seek temporary relief from principal payments. To get relief, the company must demonstrate that it has the ability to meet its interest payments and that it has a strategy for returning to higher profits in the near future.

Banks are receptive to this approach *if* the strategy for returning to profitability makes sense *and* they have reasonable assurance that they'll get their interest payments on time. The times interest earned ratio helps bankers evaluate a company's ability to make its interest payments on time. Here's the ratio:

$$\frac{\text{Income before income taxes} + \text{Interest expense}}{\text{Interest expense}}$$

As you can see, it's exactly the same as the debt service coverage ratio except that we've eliminated the principal payments from the denominator. In this way, you can determine how readily the company can make its interest payments from profits. The target for this ratio is 2 to 1 (two dollars of profit for every dollar of interest expense) or better. If your company's profits aren't adequate to meet your debt service requirements, the times interest earned ratio can help you evaluate the likelihood that your bank will work with you during this difficult period.

Leverage ratios offer insights into the financing risk a company is assuming, its borrowing capacity and how well it can afford the debt it currently owes/desires.

Now, let's turn our attention to the profitability ratios.

Profitability ratios

Profitability ratios help us discern trends in profitability, trends that aren't always obvious from reading the income statement. Here's an example to illustrate this point.

You're comparing your company's first quarter gross profit to the first quarter of last year. Here's what the income statement shows:

	Quarter ending	
	3/31/03	**3/31/02**
Sales	11,837,536	10,476,920
Cost of sales	8,049,524	6,914,767
Gross profit	3,788,012	3,562,153

On the surface, it appears that your company is doing well; both the revenues and gross profit are increasing. Yet, when we calculate the gross profit percentage (our first profitability ratio), we find that gross profit margins dropped from 34% (3,562,153/10,476,920) to 32% (3,788,012/11,837,536). Without the gross profit ratio, this trend might be overlooked.

Profitability ratios are designed to help us avoid this kind of oversight. Let's take a look at each of the profitability ratios to see how they help us identify trends and the underlying causes behind those trends.

Gross profit percentage
The gross profit percentage helps us identify trends in gross profit. The formula is:

$$\frac{\text{Gross profit}}{\text{Net sales}}$$

Gross profit represents the profit that's left after production costs (cost of goods sold/cost of sales) are covered. Gross profit is the first profit measure on the income statement.

Net sales represents total sales dollars generated for the period less amounts refunded to customers who returned merchandise (sales returns) and discounts given to customers who keep damaged/defective goods (sales allowances).

Net sales = Total sales-sales returns-sales allowances

By analyzing the trend in the gross profit percentage over months or years, you get a sense for whether the profit margins are improving or declining. If they're improving, you're obviously doing something right. Let's make sure that you know what that is so that you can continue the trend. If margins are declining, you'll want to know why so that you can reverse the trend.

There are three factors that affect gross profit. They are price, production costs and capacity utilization (sales volume). To understand what's driving the trend in gross profit, you need only investigate these three aspects of your company's operation.

If your company is experiencing improved margins it may be because you've found a way to get better prices for your offerings, reduce production costs or increase the number of units you're able to sell. Falling margins indicate that your company is experiencing price pressures, higher production costs or its unit sales volume is off. The gross profit percent ratio is designed to help you determine which of these factors is causing your success or dilemma.

For a more detailed discussion of the factors influencing gross profit see *Gross profit* on page 239. The second profitability ratio is the operating income percentage.

Operating income percentage
Operating income is the profit that's left after covering production costs and selling, general & administrative expenses (overhead). To calculate the operating income percentage, divide operating income by net sales.

> Operating income
> Net sales

When the gross profit percentage is what you targeted in your pricing, but the operating income percentage isn't, you need only focus your attention on the overhead (selling, general & administrative expenses). Why? If you refer back to Table 9.2 on page 242, you'll see that the only items between gross profit and operating income are the selling, general &

administrative expenses. That means that if gross profit is what you expected and operating income isn't the explanation has to be in the overhead costs, selling, general & administrative expenses.

Typically, you want the growth of your selling, general & administrative expenses to lag the growth in sales and gross profits. There are, however, times when you need to make an investment in the future and it makes sense for the expenses to lead the growth in sales and gross profit. For example, if your company is investing heavily in R&D (research and development) to create new offerings for the future or it's making investments to expand geographically or launching an advertising campaign to market a new offering, it makes sense that these costs will lead the revenues and gross profit you expect to generate. Otherwise, you want your overhead growth to lag sales and gross profit growth.

The third and final profitability ratio is return on sales percentage, sometimes called the net income percent.

Return on sales percentage
To calculate return on sales you divide net income by net sales.

Net income
Net sales

Net income is the profit that's left after covering production costs, overhead, extraordinary items and income taxes. In other words, it's the profit that's available to the owners. By taking this profit measure and dividing by net sales, you get a sense for how much of each dollar of revenue is left for the owners. Obviously, the higher the percentage the greater the benefit the owners are getting from their investment.

A rising return on sales percentage reflects greater operating efficiency unless the rise is attributable to extraordinary gains. Similarly, return on sales declines usually indicates less operating efficiency unless the decline is the result of an extraordinary loss. The analysis you perform using the gross profit percentage and operating income percentage will help you understand the reasons for rising/falling return on sales.

Another way to view the return on sales percentage is as a margin for error. Companies with a high return on sales percentage can take more risks than those with a low percentage. In other words, a company with 12% return on sales is more likely to survive a bad decision than one with 2% return on sales.

Profitability ratios make it easier to identify trends in profitability as well as the causes of those trends.

Before we move on to our final group of ratios, return ratios, you may have noticed that I didn't list any standards for profitability ratios as I did with the liquidity and leverage ratios. The reason is that the percentages vary widely from industry to industry. To find standards for your industry, check with your industry trade association or ask for RMA Financial Statement Studies at the reference desk of your local/college library.

Return ratios
There are two return ratios, return on assets and return on equity. Both are designed to evaluate management's effectiveness. The first return ratio is return on assets.

Return on assets

With this ratio you get a sense for how effectively assets are being employed in the business. The return on assets ratio compares a company's profit to the assets it employs in generating those profits. The formula is:

$$\frac{Net\ income\ +\ \begin{array}{c}Interest\ expense\\ net\ of\ taxes\end{array}}{Average\ total\ assets}$$

For this formula, profit is defined as net income (the income available to the owners) adjusted for financing costs (interest expense net of taxes).

The adjustment for financing costs allows us to compare our company's return on assets with returns of other companies in our industry. The financing cost adjustment recognizes the fact that every company uses a different mix of debt and equity in financing its business. Companies with high levels of debt experience higher interest costs than those that are financed primarily with equity. The easiest way to eliminate this disparity is to eliminate interest expense from the profit calculation. In essence, this ratio assumes that all companies are financed using only equity. That's why we add interest expense net of taxes to net income in the numerator. The obvious question is, "What does interest expense net of taxes mean?" I'm glad you asked.

Interest expense is deductible for income tax purposes, which means that interest expense reduces the amount of income tax a company would otherwise pay. Remember, we're trying to eliminate debt financing cost from the profit calculation. The true cost of using debt is the interest the company pays less the income tax it saves by deducting the interest. The phrase

Interest Expense Net of Taxes means interest expense minus
income tax savings. How do you calculate those tax savings?
Here's the formula:

$$\frac{\text{Income tax expense}}{\text{Income before income taxes}} \quad \text{x} \quad \text{Interest expense}$$

First, you calculate the income tax rate, that's income tax
expense divided by income before income taxes. Then you
multiply the tax rate times interest expense to get tax savings.
Using the above formula for interest expense net of taxes,
you can restate the return on assets formula as:

$$\frac{\text{Net Income} + \text{Interest expense} - (\text{Interest expense x income tax rate})}{\text{Average total assets}}$$

It shows net income as the starting profit number, adds back
the interest expense, then subtracts the tax savings on the
interest to eliminate the true cost of debt financing. While
this formula may seem cumbersome, it's necessary if you
want to make apples to apples comparisons with other
companies in your industry.

So far we've only discussed the numerator in the return on
assets ratio. Fortunately, the denominator is a much easier
concept to grasp. Average Total Assets is a simple average.
It's the total assets at the beginning of the period plus the
total assets at the end of the period, that sum divided by two.
Here's what the formula looks like:

$$\frac{\text{Total assets at beginning of period} + \text{Total assets end of period}}{2}$$

Now that we've made it through the calculations what do you do with this information? You compare your company's return on assets to the returns generated by other companies in your industry. If your company's return on assets is higher than the industry average, management is doing a better job of managing assets than many of your competitors are.

Conversely, if your company's return on assets is lower than the industry average, management is employing more assets than its competitors or not producing as much profit from those assets as its competitors are. Either way, you'll want to learn how your company can increase the returns on its assets. Why?

Companies that manage assets well have cash available to:

- Take advantage of new opportunities
- Expand geographically
- Expand into new markets by adding new offerings
- Thrive during an economic downturn

These are just a few of the reasons why you need to continuously strive for higher returns on your assets. Now let's turn our attention to the return on equity, the second return ratio.

Return on equity
Return on equity calculates the rate of return the owners are getting on their investment in the business. The formula is:

Net income
Average equity

Fortunately, this is a much simpler ratio to calculate than
return on assets. The numerator comes from the bottom line
of the income statement, no adjustments. The denominator is
a simple average, total equity at the beginning of the period
plus total equity at the end of the period, that sum divided by
2. Here's the formula:

$$\frac{\text{Total equity} \qquad \text{Total equity}}{\text{beginning of period} + \text{end of period}}$$
$$2$$

With this ratio we're comparing profits (net income) with the
owners' investment (equity). Just as with the Return on
Assets, you'll want to compare your company's results with
those of your competitors, but that isn't the end of the story.
You'll also compare your company's return on equity with
other investments available to your owners. Why? Because
they're making that comparison!

Let's assume that your company is providing a 7% return on
equity; in other words, the company's bottom line profit is
7% of the owners' investment. Let's also assume that United
States Treasury Bills are currently paying 6%. As an
investor, which investment would you choose?

Many of us would look at the virtually risk-free T-bill
investment, then look at the risk associated with running a
business and decide that 1% wasn't adequate compensation
for the additional risk. In a situation like this, the company is
going to find it difficult to attract equity investment should it
need it. That's the reason why management needs to focus
on ways of increasing return on equity for its owners.

Return ratios are designed to measure management's effectiveness in managing assets and providing adequate compensation for the risk owners are taking.

Whew! We finally completed the ratios. I know that this chapter is much longer than the others and I appreciate your perseverance. Before we move on to our next chapter, *Administration*, I'd like to share with you some common misconceptions about finance.

Other Misconceptions
In recent years, there are a couple of areas of accounting that have been challenged, cost accounting and return on equity. Let's see what the critics have to say.

Cost Accounting
There are two alternative approaches to traditional cost accounting that have been proposed in recent years. They are Activity-Based Management (ABM) and the Theory of Constraints. Let's explore ABM first.

ABM
Traditional cost accounting measures the profitability of a product line/service offering by comparing production costs with sales. If a product is sold for $1.00 and the cost to produce it was $.60, the profit on that product is $.40 or 40% of the sale price.

Proponents of Activity-Based Management (ABM) argue that the $.40 profit number in the example above is misleading. Why? It doesn't include the marketing, selling or general & administrative costs associated with this product. ABM proponents argue that the cost of marketing and selling can be dramatically different for each product/service offering.

One of your offerings may require elaborate presentations and numerous meetings with a variety of committees before an order is received. Other offerings may only require a phone call and one follow-up meeting to generate the order. The selling costs for these two offerings are dramatically different. ABM suggests that these differences in marketing and selling costs be included when measuring each offering's true profitability.

ABM makes the same argument for administration costs. The amount spent on procurement, invoicing the customer, collecting the receivable and doing the bookkeeping can vary widely. For example, the bookkeeping for a company whose typical order is $100,000 is considerably less that one whose average order is $100. If each company generates $100,000 in sales, the first company is issuing one invoice while the second is issuing 1,000 invoices.

Proponents of ABM argue that all costs involved in getting an order, procuring materials, invoicing, collecting as well as other administrative costs must be considered to get a true measure of profitability for each offering. This approach makes sense and I highly recommend that you use it in addition to the traditional cost accounting approach. Why do I say "in addition to" traditional cost accounting? I believe that there are insights to be gained from every approach you use in analyzing your company's numbers.

Note: Chapter 6, *Production*, includes a more detailed discussion of ABM. Now let's explore the Theory of Constraints' criticism of traditional cost accounting.

Theory of Constraints

Traditional cost accounting measures cost per unit of production for each stage of the production process. Let's say that a product goes through three processes, each on a different machine before it's finally complete.

Machine A	Machine B	Machine C
30 units/hour	35 units per hour	27 units per hour

For each step in the process, traditional cost accounting calculates a cost per unit based on the number of units produced. Naturally, the more units produced the lower the cost per unit. Using the process above, if Machine A costs $150/hour to run and it produces 10 units, the cost per unit is $15 ($150/10 units). If Machine A produces 30 units, its cost is $5 per unit ($150/30 units).

When cost is viewed this way, the natural inclination is to operate each machine to its capacity to keep the cost per unit as low as possible. Unfortunately, this calculation overlooks some significant costs, costs associated with the inventory build up this approach fosters. Here's what happens.

Using the production process described above, let's say that a customer orders 27 units, the exact number Machine C can produce. That means that each machine need produce only 27 units to meet demand.

If, however, management's goal is to drive down production cost per unit, it's going to have Machine A produce 30 units and Machine C produce 35 units. The excess production, 3 units for Machine A (30-27) and 8 units (35-27) for Machine B, becomes inventory.

This inventory has to be stored, insured, handled multiple times and may even be lost through obsolescence, theft or accident. Yet these costs are not considered in determining the cost per unit. What's the answer to this dilemma?

First, make sure that customer orders are driving your production activity, not cost per unit. Second, use the higher cost per unit to drive you to explore alternative production methods (see Chapter 6, *Production*), alternative markets to serve or a combination of the two.

Theory of Constraints and ABM offer valid criticisms of traditional cost accounting; incorporate these approaches in the analysis of your company's results.

With these discoveries under our belts, let's turn our attention to Return on Equity.

Return On Equity

In recent years there has been a strong movement, especially within Fortune 500 companies, to gain greater insights into what drives stock values. The managements of these companies realize that it is their job to produce increasingly higher returns for the owners (stockholders). These returns include both higher profits and greater stock values.

In response to this need, two premier consulting firms have offered approaches for increasing investor returns. Stern Stewart & Co. offers Economic Value Added (EVA) as an approach to creating value for owners. McKinsey & Company, Inc. offers Value Based Management (VBM).

These approaches are very similar so I'll highlight only the similarities. If you want to learn more about these two approaches to creating shareholder value, I refer you to:

> **The Quest for Value**
> G. Bennett Stewart, III
> HarperCollins 1991
>
> **Valuation**
> Tom Copeland, Tim Koller, Jack Murrin
> John Wiley & Sons, Inc. 1995

Both EVA and VBM focus on cash flow rather than profits as a measure of return. They suggest that senior management should base their decisions on the amount of cash their investments are expected to generate rather than the short-term profit impact, that the cash flow focus will drive stock values higher than the profit focus. Here's an example to illustrate their point.

During difficult economic times many companies postpone employee training. Why? Training costs are expensed in the income statement which makes the short-term profit picture even more dismal than it already is.

EVA and VBM both suggest that short-term profit impact is a short-sighted view. For example, they suggest that employee training is an investment in the future; consequently, the criteria for investing in training are the amount of cash that the company can expect to generate as a result of a more productive workforce and the cost of training. There is obvious merit to this argument.

Both EVA and VBM suggest modifications to the way that income statement and balance sheet accounts are stated so that they reflect more accurately the long-term impact on cash. They suggest that it is more appropriate to list training costs as an investment on the balance sheet rather than expensing it in the income statement. The return on that training investment would be determined by measuring the additional cash flow it generates vis-à-vis greater employee productivity and improved quality/customer service.

By focusing management energies on long-term cash flow rather than short-term profit goals, EVA and VBM believe that the value of the owners' investment (the value of the stock) increases more rapidly. I agree with a lot of what EVA and VBM offer, but I also have some concerns.

Caveat
EVA suggests an aggressive use of debt for enhancing shareholder returns. We know from our discussion of the leverage ratios above that we can increase returns by using debt. EVA suggests that borrowing aggressively gives management an additional incentive to perform, that higher monthly debt payments force management to perform.

I have two concerns with that philosophy. First, while it's true that some management teams excel under pressure, others may become so overwhelmed that they virtually cease to function at all. Before embarking on an aggressive borrowing strategy, assess management's temperament for this kind of stress. Second, I believe it's prudent to keep some cash flow cushion for inevitable economic downturns.

Finally, additional cash flow created through better decisions doesn't always translate into higher stock prices. In 2003, we faced a lot of uncertainty in the world, terrorism, war, industry consolidations, rising U.S. deficits and lackluster demand in most of the world's major markets.

All of these factors influence investor behavior and stock prices. Even companies who employ EVA or VBM have experienced significant declines in the value of their stock over the past 3 years. I'm not suggesting that you abandon EVA or VBM, but they are not panaceas for what ails a down stock market. Both EVA and VBM have a lot to offer; just don't expect them to solve all your problems.

Once again, we've covered a lot of material. Let's take a moment and reflect on what we've learned.

Concept – Finance

> **You want your finance function to provide the information your operations people need to make informed, balanced decisions.**

Executive Summary – Finance

- A balanced decision is one that optimizes the impact a transaction has on *all three financial statements*, the balance sheet, income statement, cash flow statement.

- The balance sheet offers insights into the company's:
  1. liquidity (its ability to pay its bills on time)
  2. financing risk (amount of debt vs. amount of equity) employed in financing its business
  3. financing capabilities (how assets can be converted to cash when needed)

- The income statement shows several different profit measures, gross profit, operating income, income before taxes and net income. Having these different profit measures allows us to narrow our field of inquiry when the results aren't what we expect.

- The cash flow statement shows the sources and uses of cash in three categories:
  1. Cash from operating activities (profits)
  2. Cash from investing activities (purchase/sale of assets)
  3. Cash from financing activities (debt/equity activities)

- Ratios offer another perspective on the numbers shown in the financial statements.

- Activity-Based Cost Management and Theory of Constraints offer alternative ways of looking at traditional cost accounting measures of unit cost.

- Economic Value Added and Value Based Management suggest that cash flow is more important than profits in increasing shareholder value.

The final chapter, *Administration*, helps us determine how we should deal with the inevitable paperwork every business faces. Join me on this, the final segment, of our journey.

ADMINISTRATION:

Contributing Factor

or

Necessary Evil?

10

Administration

What is the key to effectively handling the myriad regulatory and administrative requirements facing your company?

To outsource any administrative work that doesn't enhance the customer experience or contribute to the bottom line.

Core Concept – Contribution

How's that law degree coming? What's that? You aren't working on a law degree. You have no interest in the law! Then you may want to rethink your decision about owning your own business or becoming a professional manager.

One of the harshest realities of business is that there are countless regulations with which you must be familiar. Remember the old adage, "Ignorance of the law excuses no man (or woman)."

There are regulations to cover virtually every aspect of business. Here are just a few examples. Regulations can:

- limit the claims you make in your marketing materials
- require disclosures in your marketing materials
- void a sales contract or limit its enforcement
- prevent you from asking certain questions or using certain tests during employee interviews
- influence how you compensate your employees
- dictate how you'll administer your retirement programs
- make it difficult to fire problem employees
- dictate insurance requirements and claims reporting as with workman's compensation insurance
- impact production processes (environmental regulations)
- impose responsibility for collecting and remitting taxes to a taxing authority
- impose tax expenses on your organization

Again, these are just a few examples of the countless regulations your company faces.

Disheartening isn't it? It is and, yet, in many instances business leaders have invited these regulations. Our predecessors invited workmen's compensation laws by not providing a safe work environment. Environmental rules were invited by careless disregard for our natural resources. Recently, Certified Public Accountants invited the Sarbanes-Oxley Act and the Public Company Accounting Oversight Board by virtue of their inability to police themselves, as evidenced by the Enron and WorldCom fiascos.

Regardless of who opened the door, your company is facing a plethora of regulations. The question is, "What's the best way to deal with them?"

There are two obvious options, ignore them or comply. If you're surprised that I'd even mention the possibility of ignoring the law, you've come to know me well. Yet, the reality is that hardly a day goes by without word of another company being investigated for violating a law or regulation. The evidence is overwhelming; owners and managers of companies around the globe are making the decision to ignore the rules. That's why I think it's imperative that we consider that option.

Ignore

I'm not suggesting that the decision to ignore the rules is made lightly. Often owners/managers perform a crude probability analysis. They weigh the odds of getting caught and its attendant penalties against the cost of compliance. If the odds of getting caught are low or the penalties are small, they often choose to ignore the rules. This is a short-sighted view for several reasons.

First, the price of getting caught is often much higher than the stated penalties. There's damage to the company's reputation which may cause it to lose customers and key employees.

Owners and managers who ignore the rules load competitors' guns for them. They invite competitors to fire salvo after salvo of negative publicity against their organization.

Second, any flexibility you may have had in determining how to comply with the law goes away. Requirements imposed on violators by regulators are usually more severe and costly than voluntary compliance.

Third, as we've already discussed, leaders who ignore the rules invite further scrutiny, not just for themselves, but for the entire business community. This scrutiny usually results in more regulation and higher costs for everyone.

These are three very good reasons why ignoring the rules should not be an option any business leader would consider.

Comply

Comply is a simple word with very complex implications. It would be nice to think that we could simply follow a regulation as promulgated and be done with it. That's just not the way the world works. Regulations are challenged, interpreted, refined and tested in court year after year after year. It's this evolutionary process that requires constant monitoring and attention to assure that compliance, once established, is maintained. The question is, "How do we best monitor the ever-changing regulatory landscape and assure continued compliance?"

Again, we have two options; we can handle compliance internally or outsource it. Let's explore the advantages and disadvantages of each approach.

Internal vs. outsource

Wow! How lucky can you get? Your company just launched a product which involves a chemical process that subjects it to a new set of environmental regulations and reporting requirements AND your boss decided that you're the right person for the job. Congratulations! How are you going to handle these new responsibilities? We'll assume that your desire to lob this hot potato onto someone else's plate died with the recollection of the boss's allusion to "holding you personally responsible."

Once you get a feel for the regulations, you're likely to consider the following factors for dealing with them.

- Organizational knowledge
- Organizational skill
- Time requirements
- Regulatory change frequency
- Budget
- Convenience

There is nothing magical about the sequence of this list. It is not my intent to suggest a sequence or the weight that should be given to each factor. I'm merely laying the groundwork for a discussion of how each of these factors might influence your decisions.

Organizational knowledge

Is anyone in your organization familiar with these regulations or the agency itself? If so, does that person know anyone in the agency who can guide him on issues that aren't clearly addressed in the regulations? What other responsibilities does this person have? Will those responsibilities get in the way of his ability to assure ongoing compliance?

If the knowledge doesn't exist in your organization, how much time, energy and money will it take to develop that knowledge? What's the cost of a misstep? What would it cost to hire an employee who possesses this knowledge? What would it cost to outsource these responsibilities?

Organizational skill
Even if someone is familiar with the regulations, does he possess the skills necessary to implement them? Just because someone knows the rules doesn't mean that he has the leadership skills to implement them. Here's an example to demonstrate my point.

I understand the mechanics of golf. I've even helped other golfers correct their problems. Yet, I can't seem to apply the mechanics well enough to effect a less than embarrassing result for myself.

Just as I have difficulty making good golf shots, your company may find it difficult to achieve compliance unless it possesses both organizational knowledge and skill. Even when both exist, you have to ask whether there are better uses of your employees' time and talents.

Time requirements
There are two different types of time investment required with regulatory compliance:

1. the initial time investment which involves establishing policies and procedures
2. the ongoing monitoring and reporting requirements that all regulatory compliance requires

There are several ways to deal with these time requirements:

- Keep the compliance entirely in-house and make the necessary time investments
- Outsource the establishment of policies and procedures and keep the ongoing monitoring and reporting in-house
- Establish the policies and procedures yourself and outsource the ongoing monitoring and reporting
- Outsource the entire effort

Before establishing your own policies and procedures, ask, "Are we reinventing the wheel?" "Can we get templates that can help us create the policies and procedures we need?" When considering these questions, don't overlook *The Uniqueness Myth*, the natural inclination to think that your business is different. Certainly, there are nuances to your business, but generally you'll find it less time consuming and less expensive to modify an existing template than to create policies and procedures from scratch.

When deciding whether to establish in-house systems to monitor compliance, consider the following questions.

- What other responsibilities do these employees have? Do these employees view their other responsibilities as being more or less important than monitoring compliance? If they consider their other duties more important, how likely are they to let their monitoring duties slide to meet these other responsibilities?
- How effective is self-monitoring? Do the designated employees have enough influence and support within the company to enforce compliance? Would an independent monitoring service have more influence

and a greater likelihood of assuring that the company remains in compliance?

- Is an outside monitoring service more likely to stay abreast of regulatory changes? If so, are they also more likely to offer a broader array of compliance options than you might discover on your own?

These are all factors to consider when evaluating the time required to monitor your company's compliance. Regulatory reporting requirements beg similar questions.

- How often are you required to report?
- How often do the rules change?
- How often do the forms change?
- How much time will it take to keep abreast of the rules and reporting form changes?
- Can you avoid some of the risk by having outsiders handle the reporting?
- Can you use your employees' time in ways that would be of greater benefit to your company?

As you can see, there are a lot of questions to be answered before you can accurately assess the time requirements for establishing policies and procedures, monitoring your company's compliance and filing the requisite reports.

You may have noticed in the questions above that we've alluded to yet another factor in the "internal vs. outsource" decision. That factor is the frequency of regulatory change.

Regulatory change frequency
Two questions asked in the last section, "How often do the rules change?" and "How often do the forms change?" help

you focus on the rate of regulatory change. The more frequently interpretations, clarifications, corrections and court cases are published, the more time your employees will have to invest to assure continued compliance. Is this a worthwhile investment of your employees' time? Is it a good investment of the payroll dollars you're expending for these people? These questions bring us to our fifth factor, budget.

Budget
Everything we do has budget implications. Is it cheaper to hire the requisite compliance services or maintain them in-house? How do you measure the cost of in-house services? This may seem like a simple question, but it's not.

The true cost goes well beyond the payroll cost of additional employees, as you'll see when you read the *Often Overlooked Factors* section below. Before we move onto that section, let's explore the sixth factor influencing our "internal vs. outsource" decision, convenience.

Convenience
Even if you possess the necessary knowledge and skills and you conclude that it's cheaper to handle compliance in-house, it may be wise to outsource it. Why? Convenience!

You may find that compliance work is something that neither you nor anyone in your organization enjoys. Lack of interest increases the likelihood of error or worse, neglect. If neither you nor your employees enjoy compliance work, outsource the work and avoid the risk.

The six factors which often determine whether to outsource compliance or maintain it in-house are organizational knowledge, organizational skill, time requirements, regulatory change frequency, budget and convenience.

Are these the right criteria to consider? They are important, but there are two often overlooked factors that I believe are of greater import. Let's see what they are.

Often Overlooked Factors

You're way ahead of me aren't you? You recall the two items I mentioned at the very beginning of this chapter, enhancing the customer experience or improving the bottom line. These should be the two most critical factors considered in your "internal vs. outsource" decision.

The cost of compliance can be much more than the cost of the employees involved. If compliance work distracts your employees from serving your customers or keeps them from exploring ways to improve your bottom line, the greater cost is lost profits.

There are times when keeping a compliance task in-house enhances your company's ability to serve its customers and improve its bottom line. For many years, a construction client kept its payroll in-house. Why? That's a good question, especially in light of the fact that most payroll services:

- prepare payroll checks
- keep abreast of changing payroll tax rules
- keep their software updated for the rule changes
- prepare reports to the various taxing authorities
- disburse funds to taxing authorities
- absorb any penalties the client firm experiences resulting from an error the payroll service made
- offer a wide array of management reports

My client kept its payroll in-house to get quicker feedback on its labor costs. The company's leaders used that information to improve the customer's experience and the bottom line. Here's how they did it.

Customer experience

The estimators got daily feedback on the labor costs on the jobs that were in progress. The information they gleaned from the payroll data allowed them to evaluate the cost of various approaches used in performing the work. This knowledge made it possible for the estimators to offer their customers options on how the work could be done.

The estimators were also able to communicate the advantages and disadvantages of each option so that the customer could evaluate each benefit against its cost. This approach helped customers make more informed decisions which added to their satisfaction with the work my client performed.

The daily labor cost feedback also allowed estimators to adjust their bidding practices more quickly, enabling them to become more accurate in their estimates of the work being done. This means that there were fewer instances where they were going back to the customer to get paid for "extras," an all too common occurrence and the source of many customer complaints in the construction industry. By eliminating the seemingly endless negotiations that occur at the end of a project, my client enhanced its customers' experiences.

My client has found that its customers are willing to pay a slightly higher price for the ability to make more informed decisions and avoid haggling over the bill. They've also found that they're garnering a larger share of the market as a result of these efforts.

You may have noticed that I used the past tense in talking about my client keeping payroll in-house. The software that exists today affords other means of monitoring their labor costs which allows them to outsource their payroll, gaining all the advantages an external service affords.

We've seen that enhancing the customer experience can improve a company's profits. There are also bottom line gains to be gotten from better cost control. Here are some of the benefits my client earned on the cost side of the equation.

Bottom line improvement
In addition to the increased sales volume and higher prices, my client assured greater consistency on the cost side of the equation. Estimators were able to minimize cost overruns by providing quick feedback to the field leaders, allowing them to adapt their approaches quickly. Daily feedback also improved estimators' ability to estimate the cost side of the work and adapt their formulas more quickly than if they were getting the typical end-of-month reports. I love gaining multiple benefits from one activity, don't you?

There is one more factor to consider in an "internal vs. outsource" decision and it's purely psychological. It, too, has the potential of affecting both the customer experience and the bottom line. Have I piqued your curiosity?

Compliance psychology
You've spent the last two months developing an idea that's going to save your company 3/4 of a million dollars. You present the idea to senior management and they *love* it. The compliance officer gets wind of your plan and throws one obstacle after another in your way, citing various regulations that won't permit your idea to work. What are you feeling?

Would you like to throttle the compliance officer? Could your feelings be expressed in polite company? Do you consider him a naysayer or deal killer? Now, place yourself in the shoes of the compliance officer. Ready?

You just saved your company more in fines, legal fees and bad publicity than the 3/4 of a million this harebrained scheme would have saved. Is anyone congratulating you for your efforts? No? What's that? You're the butt of disparaging jokes and nasty comments. How unfair.

Let's be honest; operating managers at all levels clash with compliance officers. The result is often disdain for each other. Operating managers view compliance people as obstacles to progress; consequently, they don't value compliance people. Compliance officers view operating managers as people who carelessly ignore the rules and potential consequences. This internal conflict creates a lot of resentment, especially on the part of the compliance people.

To understand the resentment compliance people experience, imagine yourself in a position where you aren't valued. What would you do? Would you try to demonstrate your value to the organization? Would you strive to make a name for yourself in hopes of gaining recognition and acceptance? And when these approaches don't work, when you realize that no matter what you do you're going to be viewed as an obstacle to progress, what do you do?

In all likelihood, you're not viewed as operating manager material because you're so "negative." That leaves you with the role of compliance officer. Many people who find themselves in this situation become more stringent in their application of the rules. They look for ways to say "No!"

They create their own fiefdom in an attempt to achieve some personal satisfaction from the job.

It's this "lord of the land" mentality that results in policies that negatively affect customer relations. This isn't limited to compliance people. Accountants, human resource people and attorneys inside organizations often experience the treatment just described. Their reaction is much the same.

It would be interesting to know who at the Bank of America decided that having tellers was expensive and that BOA should charge a $3 fee to anyone who wanted the services of a teller. What a wonderful way to tell the customer he's a nuisance. By the way, Bank of America has abandoned that policy and has created a friendlier, more enjoyable teller experience for its customers.

Driving customers away isn't the only way unappreciated employees affect the bottom line. They also develop a plethora of policies that make work more complex and expensive for the organization. Remember, they're striving for recognition. The more elaborate the policy of protection, the more important they are (at least in their eyes).

Compliance psychology often results in policies that diminish the customer experience or reduce the bottom line. At its zenith, compliance psychology can accomplish both.

You may be asking yourself, "Doesn't that same psychology exist in outsourced services?" Typically not. Providers of outsourced services realize that management:

- views the outsourced service as a necessary evil
- desires to minimize the cost of these activities

- want these services to be seamless with their other operating activities
- expect the provider to find ways for operating managers to achieve their goals while maintaining compliance with all existing regulations

In fact, the providers of these services are selling these benefits to management. That's why their businesses are so successful. Here's a quick suggestion for those of you who enjoy compliance work: find employment with an outsource compliance provider. Here's what you can gain by working for an outsource firm:

- greater recognition for the value you provide
- higher compensation than you would typically make inside a client organization
- greater job security; you're not as likely to be subjected to economic swings in an outsource operation as you are in client organizations that tend to bring these services in-house in good times, then quickly abandon them when times are difficult

Compliance work is valuable work. For those of you with an interest in that work, I hope these suggestions help you achieve a more enjoyable and financially rewarding career.

Our discussion has been about compliance matters. There is also a misconception that some non-compliance activities are essential to your business. Let's see what activities those are.

Other Misconceptions

There are a myriad of outsource services that make a lot of sense even though they aren't compliance related. Let's be honest; there are some activities in which we simply aren't involved frequently enough to develop the skills to do the job well. While this list is by no means all-inclusive, here are some of those activities:

- Staffing
- Compensation
- Temporary staffing
- Relocation
- Expatriation
- Information technology
- Public relations
- Multi-state tax services
- Investment advice
- Outplacement services
- Risk assessment/management

Activity	Benefits from Outsourcing
Staffing	Staffing firms are more familiar with the various testing tools available and how to employ them legally; they are also more adept at interviewing and references checking
Compensation	Compensation firms have the tools and independence to survey the market; they are more aware of trends in compensation and the legalities of complex pay packages

Activity	Benefits from Outsourcing
Temporary staffing	Temporary help firms have a large pool of workers from which to draw; the workers have generally been tested; the temporary staffing firms know their workers' capabilities, work ethic and performance from other temporary assignments which allows them to do a better job of meeting your temporary staffing needs
Relocation	These firms make it easier for you, your employees and their families to deal with the stress of job-related moves by helping the employee and his family become familiar with their new community, referring them to resources in the community and helping them understand the real estate market
Expatriation	Relocations to countries outside the home country pose additional problems including language, culture, customs, business climate and business practices; expatriation services provide insights which often don't exist within your company

Activity	Benefits from Outsourcing
Information technology	Even some of the Fortune 500 are outsourcing their IT systems management efforts; the rate of change in technology makes it difficult for many companies to stay abreast of the changes and expensive to keep their systems up-to-date
Public relations	Few companies have people on staff with the media contacts to assure timely placement of press releases; this makes it difficult to tout their successes or rebut negative publicity; public relations firms are in the business of nurturing the media relationships necessary to achieve these goals
Multi-state tax services	These organizations keep you abreast of changing tax laws and registration requirements in all of the states in which your company operates
Investment advice	Important whether retirement plan investments are company or employee directed

Activity	Benefits from Outsourcing
Outplacement services	Career assistance for employees whose services the company no longer desires
Risk assessment/management	These firms have the math skills and an ear for risk that enables them to help you identify and evaluate the risk in your plans

Again, this is not an all-inclusive list; rather it is intended to demonstrate that there are activities in virtually every area of the operation that could (probably should) be outsourced.

When evaluating the work your operating managers are performing, ask yourself, "Are these managers regularly involved in and skilled at these types of activities?" If not, consider outsourcing the work.

Many business owners/leaders are looking at the professional functions within their organizations, accountants, human resource professionals and in-house counsel, to determine whether these functions should be outsourced. Given what we know about compliance psychology, it's a valid question.

It's time for our final review. Let's take a moment to recall the key considerations for dealing with administration.

Core Concept – Administration

The key to effectively handling the regulatory and administrative requirements facing your company is to outsource any work that doesn't enhance the customer experience or contribute to the bottom line.

Executive Summary – Administration

- There are compliance issues related to virtually every aspect of business.

- Ignoring the rules has costs well beyond the potential fines you might have to pay. These costs include:

  1. Damage to the company's reputation which can translate into loss of customers and key employees
  2. Flexibility in deciding how to comply with the rules
  3. An invitation to more scrutiny and further regulation with its attendant costs

- Compliance can be managed internally or outsourced. The factors usually considered in this decision are:

  1. Organizational knowledge
  2. Organizational skill
  3. Time requirements
  4. Regulatory change frequency
  5. Budget
  6. Convenience

- Compliance psychology, the tendency of management to undervalue compliance, often results in compliance people establishing fiefdoms with unfortunate consequences for both the customer experience and the bottom line.

- Handling compliance in-house makes sense if it helps the company enhance the customers' experience or improves the bottom line.

- Some duties are performed so infrequently that we don't have an opportunity to become truly skilled in their performance; it's wise to outsource these duties.

AUTHOR'S NOTE:

Author's Note

There are a couple of observations about *The Uniqueness Myth* that I'd like to share with you.

First, my darling wife, Charlotte, who is a wonderfully observant proof reader, noted that this is an ethical book. While that was not my intent, I am happy to have achieved that result. I would like to share with you what business ethics does for me.

1. It simplifies my life. I don't have to think about which "strategy" I'm employing; it's always the one that offers the greatest benefit to all parties involved.
2. Business ethics protects me from people who would take advantage of me. It's difficult for others to argue against my position when it's one that benefits all parties to the transaction.
3. I enjoy long-term relationships with my clients, in part, because they enjoy dealing with someone who has their best interests at heart; someone who speaks openly and candidly with them.

Second, Charlotte observed that *The Uniqueness Myth* describes a utopian environment. Indeed, I know that Chapters 4, *Customer Service*, and 8, *Work Environment*, portray the ideal environment for customers and employees. Yet, shouldn't we be continuously striving for these ideals? Should the fact that our humanity won't allow us to achieve perfection dissuade us from moving ever closer to it?

My experience and that of my clients has been that work is more enjoyable *and* financially rewarding as we get closer to perfection. My wish for you is that today you begin your journey to utopia, enjoying all the rewards that never-ending adventure affords.

Dale Furtwengler

Bibliography

This bibliography is presented to save you time in locating one of the many book references I've made.

Management
Patrick Kelly, *Faster Company*, Wiley & Sons 1998

Andrew S. Grove, *Only the Paranoid Survive*, Doubleday, October 1996

Marketing
Jay Conrad Levinson, *Guerilla Marketing*, Houghton Mifflin 1984

Michael Treacy & Fred Wiersema, *The Discipline of Market Leaders*, Addison-Wesley Publishing, 1995

Selling
Robert Ringer, *Winning Through Intimidation*, Los Angeles Book Publishing, 1974

Tom Hopkins, *How to Master the Art of Selling*, Warner Books, 1982

Barabara Geraghty, *Visionary Selling*, Simon & Schuster, 1998

Jeffrey Gitomer, *The Sales Bible*, William Morrow, HarperCollins

Quality/Production
Michael Hammer & James Champy, *Reengineering the Corporation: A Manifesto for Business Revolution*, HarperBusiness, 1993

Eliyahu Goldratt, *The Goal*, The North River Press, 1984, 1986, 1992

Eliyahu Goldratt, *Necessary But Not Sufficient*, The North River Press, 2000

James Womack & Daniel Jones, *Lean Thinking*, Simon & Schuster, 1996

Christopher E. Bogan and Michael J. English, *Benchmarking For Best Practices*, McGraw-Hill 1994

Robin Cooper, Robert S. Kaplan, Lawrence S. Maisel, Eileen Morrissey and Ronald M. Oehm, *Implementing Activity-Based Cost Management*, Institute of Management Accountants 1992

Peter Pande, Robert Neuman, Roland Cavanagh, *The Six Sigma Way*, McGraw-Hill 2000

Michael L. George, *Lean Six Sigma*, McGraw-Hill 2002

Organizational Structure
Elliott Jaques, *Requisite Organization*, Cason Hall, 1997

Work Environment
Kenneth Blanchard, *Raving Fans: A Revolutionary Approach to Customer Service,* William Morrow & Co. 1993

Dale Furtwengler, *Making the Exceptional Normal*, Peregrine Press 1997

Lance A. Berger and Dorothy R. Berger – Editors in Chief, *The Compensation Handbook: A State-of-the-Art Guide to Compensation Strategy and Design*, McGraw Hill, Fourth Edition

Robert J. Doyle, Jr., *Gainsharing and Productivity: A Guide to Planning, Implementation, and Development*, Anacom 1983

Finance
G. Bennett Stewart, III, *The Quest for Value*, HarperCollins 1991

Tom Copeland, Tim Koller, Jack Murrin, *Valuation,* John Wiley & Sons, Inc. 1995

Index

About the Author

Dale Furtwengler has authored three other books and dozens of articles. His books include:

Making the EXCEPTIONAL Normal
Peregrine Press, 1997

The 10-Minute Guide to Performance Appraisals
Macmillan USA, 2000

Living Your Dreams
Peregrine Press, 2001

Some of his more popular articles are:

Tips for Crafting Your 30-Second "Elevator Speech"
Increase Profits Without Adding Resources (series)
...but your price is too high!
If We Lose One More Top Performer...
Making the EXCEPTIONAL Normal (series)

You can find more information on these books and articles at Dale's website at:

www.furtwengler.com.